COLLEGE AND UNIVERSITY BANDS

Their Organization and Administration

BY

L. V. BUCKTON

SUBMITTED IN PARTIAL FULFILLMENT OF THE REQUIREMENTS FOR
THE DEGREE OF DOCTOR OF PHILOSOPHY IN THE FACULTY
OF PHILOSOPHY, COLUMBIA UNIVERSITY

Bureau of Publications
Teachers College, Columbia University
NEW YORK CITY
1929

COLLEGE AND UNIVERSITY BANDS

THEIR ORGANIZATION AND ADMINISTRATION

BY

L. V. BUCKTON

SUBMITTED IN PARTIAL FULFILLMENT OF THE REQUIREMENTS FOR
THE DEGREE OF DOCTOR OF PHILOSOPHY IN THE FACULTY
OF PHILOSOPHY, COLUMBIA UNIVERSITY

BUREAU OF PUBLICATIONS
Teachers College, Columbia University
NEW YORK CITY
1929

Printed in the United States of America by
J. J. LITTLE AND IVES COMPANY, NEW YORK

ACKNOWLEDGMENTS

I am deeply grateful to all who have made this study possible and who have assisted in its preparation:

To Professor Edward S. Evenden, of the Department of College Administration, Teachers College, Columbia University, who was chairman of my dissertation committee; and to the members of the committee, Professors Peter W. Dykema, of the Department of Public School Music, and Floyd B. O'Rear, of the Department of College Administration—all of whom gave freely of their time and advice.

To the bandmasters of the colleges, universities, and normal schools who furnished the data covering the present condition of band work in institutions of higher education.

To Karl B. Shuckman of the York Band Instrument Company; R. M. White of the H. N. White Company; F. E. Waters of the C. G. Conn, Ltd., Company; F. A. Holtz of the Martin Band Instrument Company; H. J. Charlton of the Frank Holton Company; and W. S. Wood, Colonel, Q. M. Corps, United States Army, for data relating to band instruments.

To the Lilley Company, Alexander D'Angelo Company, National Uniform Company, De Moulin Brothers and Company, and Stone Uniform Company for data relating to band uniforms.

To the National Bureau for the Advancement of Music for many helpful suggestions.

To Miss Adrienne Moukad for her efficient work in arranging and typing the thesis.

To my wife, Mrs. Eva Saunders Buckton, for her help in checking the tables included in the study.

L. V. B.

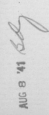

CONTENTS

COLLEGE AND UNIVERSITY BANDS

Their Organization and Administration

CHAPTER I

INTRODUCTION

Walter Damrosch says: "What America needs at this time is a band in every community." [1] This should be extended to read, What every college and university in America needs is a good band. The band has an important musical function to perform. Too often the greatest musical possibilities of the band have not been realized. "At its best the band is a very fine musical organization. The complete concert band has as great a variety of tonal color and contrast as the orchestra." [2] E. W. Goldman says: "I personally believe that the concert band of the future will be the equal, if not the superior, in artistic effects, of the symphony orchestra." [3]

Two distinct types of bands are recognized, the military band and the symphonic or concert band, both of which have a distinct function in the college or university. Standards for a symphonic band have already been set forth in connection with public school bands. [4] High standards of attainment have been set forth particularly for concert bands. [5] One reason the symphonic or concert band has not been developed to the highest perfection is the lack of instruments. "If the desired instrument is available, it is not difficult to get the player." [6]

The place of the band in the social and extra-curricular life of the institution may be seen from Tables VI and VII. Here

[1] Byrn, Clarence, "The School Band—an Educational Institution." *Jacobs Band Monthly,* Jan. 1926, pp. 3-7.
[2] Grabel, V. J., "The Band as an Important Musical Factor." *The Etude,* Vol. 46, Jan., Feb. 1928, pp. 31, 115.
[3] Eisenberg, Jacob, " 'Let Us Have a Good Brass Band in Every Community,' Says Goldman." *The Musician,* 32 : 11, April 1927.
[4] Maddy, J. E., "How to Develop a School Band." *The Etude,* 44 : 424, June 1926.
[5] Grabel, V. J., "Ideals in Band Performance (Preparing for Contests and Concerts)." *The Etude,* 46 : 367, May 1928.
[6] Woods, G. H., *Public School Orchestras and Bands.* Oliver Ditson Co., Boston, 1922, p. 104.

it will be noted that the bands, at the 54 institutions studied, played for 2,636 functions during the year 1926-1927. In all there were 3,565 men and 169 women, without duplication, engaged in band work at these institutions.

The value of a band in developing "school spirit" or *esprit de corps* has long been recognized. Industries have long recognized the value of a good band. "Including letter carriers', firemen's, policemen's and others the number of employee bands in the United States will probably reach one thousand. The value of equipment would be well over $3,500,000 for these bands." [7] The value of bands in this connection during war time was generally recognized in training camps overseas and in various drives at home. [8] The function of a band in a college or university in this phase is no less important.

A band also has an educational value which should be considered. Dr. P. P. Claxton, former Commissioner of Education, says: "Sooner or later we shall not only recognize the cultural value of music—we shall also begin to understand that, after the beginnings of reading, writing, arithmetic, and geography, music has greater practical value than any other subject taught in our schools." [9] Dr. Charles W. Eliot, for many years President of Harvard University, said, "Music rightly taught is the best mind trainer on the list." [10] "Positive proof that music is the best mind trainer has come from Magdalen College, where all the musical instruction at Oxford University is given. There are many prizes and scholarships. Only ten per cent of the students at Magdalen take music; yet this ten per cent take seventy-five per cent of all those prizes and scholarships, leaving only twenty-five per cent for the other ninety per cent of the students. This is not the record of one year, but the average of thirty successive years." [11]

"The school band possesses all the advantages of athletics: deep breathing, physical and mental alertness, and team play.

[7] Grabel, V. J., "How American Industries Are Utilizing Music." *The Etude,* 41 : 303-4, May 1923.

[8] Boutelle, G. H., "Economic Value of Music in War." *Bellman,* 23 : 439-41, Oct. 20, 1917.

[9] Mirick, G. C., *School Bands, How to Organize and Train Them.* J. W. York, Grand Rapids, Mich., 1924, p. 4.

[10] *Ibid.*

[11] Barnes. Edwin N. C., *Music as an Educational and Social Asset.* Theodore Presser Co., 1927, p. xiii.

It also teaches the student how to plan, give, and carry out orders. It develops self-reliance and a sense of responsibility. A band student is far more likely to be able to use his acquired skill in a vocational way later on than the athlete." [12]

A good band is a fine publicity medium when used on tours, radio broadcasting, concerts, and the various activities at which a band plays both on and off the campus. Many college and university bands have a high publicity value where a fine concert organization has been developed.

The band also has a real value in developing professional and semi-professional musicians. Many students receive training that helps them defray part or all of their college expenses. Many more direct musical organizations, after they have completed college, either in the amateur or professional field. The band furnishes practical training for the development of public school music supervisors, especially in the normal schools and teachers colleges. "The effect of playing on band members may be summarized as follows: it is excellent training in discipline, directs attention to detail work and opens the doorway to professional life." [13]

[12] Byrn, Clarence, "Public School Training in Vocational Music," *Jacobs Band Monthly,* June 1926, pp. 3-7.
[13] Grabel, V. J., "Appreciation of School Bands," *The Etude,* 46 : 115, 119, Feb. 1928.

CHAPTER II

STANDARDS FOR COLLEGE AND UNIVERSITY BANDS

It was necessary to determine the present practice of college, university, and normal school and teachers college bands by means of a survey. A survey blank was prepared and checked for corrections and additions by the research group in College Administration at Teachers College, the Department of Public School Music, and eight bandmasters who were interested in the work.

The 1926 Directory of the United States Bureau of Education was consulted in order to make a list of colleges, universities, and normal schools and teachers colleges. The catalogues of these institutions were consulted in order to determine those that specified a band. Two survey blanks were sent to each bandmaster of the 101 institutions that indicated a band in their catalogue. The complete form appears in Appendix C. Complete returns were received from 54 institutions.

After a preliminary tabulation of results, made on a large table in order to get the general tendencies of practice found in the colleges and universities, a set of tentative standards for college and university bands was made out from the table covering the following points: A. Personnel, B. Equipment, C. Activities, D. Financing and Budget-making. These tentative standards represent the best practice as determined from the preliminary tabulation plus a few standards which were not common but which appeared necessary and desirable. They were checked by the dissertation committee, a member of the faculty of the Department of Public School Music, and five bandmasters before they were sent out.

A personal letter was sent to six outstanding bandmasters now in college or university work for names of outstanding bandmasters who had had college and university band experience but who are not now engaged in college band activity. A list was also made up through the Department of Public School Music which included outstanding bandmasters. From these two sources a list of 30 outstanding bandmasters who had had college or university band experience was selected to check the set of tentative standards. Care was taken to avoid duplicating institutions or bandmasters who had filled out the original survey blank. Complete returns were received from 20 of these bandmasters. The names of these directors are as follows:

1. Edwin Franko Goldman, Director The Goldman Band, New York City.
2. Ed. Chennette, Director and Composer, DeKalb, Illinois.
3. Pat Conway, Head Conway Band School, Ithaca, New York.
4. LeRoy Allen, formerly Director University of California Band, Berkeley, California.
5. W. W. Norton, Community Music Association, Flint, Michigan.
6. Clel Silvey, Bandmaster, Austin, Texas.
7. Forrest L. Buchtel, Director of Band and Orchestra, Kansas State Teachers College, Emporia, Kansas.
8. Theodore F. Fitch, University of Rochester, Rochester, New York.
9. Roy E. Freeburg, University of Montana, Missoula, Montana.
10. George L. Coleman, Cornell University, Ithaca, New York.
11. G. H. Brandes, Muhlenberg College, Allentown, Pennsylvania.
12. Carlyle Scott, Director of Music, University of Minnesota, Minneapolis, Minnesota.
13. J. Arndt Bergh, Director St. Olaf College Band, Northfield, Minnesota.
14. Adelbert W. Sprague, Director Department of Music, University of Maine, Orono, Maine.
15. Adolph Vogel, University of Pennsylvania, Philadelphia, Pennsylvania.
16. Frank T. Guilbeau, Director Louisiana State University Band, Baton Rouge, Louisiana.
17. Howard S. Monger, Director of Instrumental Music, Fresno State College, Fresno, California.
18. J. DeForest Cline, Head, Conservatory of Music, Colorado State Teachers College, Greeley, Colorado.
19. Richard J. Dunn, Director College Band, Agricultural and Mechanical College, College Station, Texas.
20. Henry Knies, Bandmaster, Nebraska Wesleyan University, Lincoln, Nebraska.

The tabulation of answers to tentative standards as checked by 20 bandmasters appears on the following pages.

A. PERSONNEL

Under the tabulation of answers to tentative standards checked by 20 bandmasters in Table I, there appears a number in the middle column which refers to the number of band-

TABLE I

TENTATIVE STANDARDS AS CHECKED BY TWENTY BANDMASTERS

TENTATIVE STANDARDS	Answers to Tentative Standards	
	Agree	Other Opinions
A. PERSONNEL		
I. The Director of the band should be a member of the Music Department of the Institution.	18	Not necessarily—2
II. The duties of the officers of the band should be clearly stated in the Constitution and By-Laws of the band.	17	Constitution and By-Laws unnecessary—1 Or R. O. T. C. Regulations—2
III. The duties of the officers of the band should be as follows: 1. DIRECTOR a) The Director should have direct charge of the band at all functions at which the band plays.	17	Should not be required to attend all student functions—2 Student Director—1
b) The Director should make requisitions through the Bursar for: (1) The purchase of new music.	17	Budget Instruments and Music—1 Approval Head Music Dept.—1 Through Purchasing Dept.—1
(2) The purchase of new instruments and supplies for the band.	17	Through Director of Music—2 Purchasing Dept.—1
(3) The repair of instruments and equipment as needed.	17	OK requisition—1 OK Head Music Dept.—1 Purchasing Dept.—1
(4) The replacement of instruments and equipment which are worn out.	18	Approval Head Music Dept.—1 Purchasing Dept.—1
(5) The purchase, replacement, and repair of uniforms as needed.	16	Approval Head Music Dept.—1 Yes, unless R. O. T. C.—2 ?—1
c) The Director should coöperate with the Business Manager in making business arrangements for all appearances of the band. The Director should be responsible for these in the final analysis.	16	?—1 Director in advisory capacity—2 If manager band member—yes ⎱—1 If faculty member　　—no ⎰
d. The Director should give instruction on Band instruments through the Music Department.	10	Not necessarily—4 If he has time—1 Or arrange for competent instruction—3 If there is a Music Dept.—2
2. STUDENT DIRECTOR a) The Student Director should be in direct charge of the band in the absence of the Director.	18	Or R. O. T. C. Officer—1 Should be member of Music Dept.—1

TABLE I—*Continued*

TENTATIVE STANDARDS	Answers to Tentative Standards	
	Agree	Other Opinions
2. STUDENT DIRECTOR—*Continued* b) The Student Director should arrange for section rehearsals.	13	Under Director's Guidance—7
c) The Student Director should take the roll of the band at rehearsals and at all functions where the band plays.	11	Or Secretary—4 Sergt. or Secretary—3 Drum Major—2
d. The Student Director should assist the Director at all times.	19	Assistant Director from Music Dept.—1
3. BUSINESS MANAGER a) The Business Manager should arrange for the transportation of men and instruments at all functions at which the band plays.	19	Captain of the band—1
b) The Business Manager should have charge of the instruments and uniforms, checking them in and out to the band members as needed.	14	Yes, unless military officer—2 Director oversee it—2 Custodians—2
c) The Business Manager should make arrangements for the Spring Tour with the help of the Director and Bursar.	17	For any tour—1 Yes, if one is taken—1 Captain and Seniors—1
d) The Business Manager should be responsible for all band equipment under the Director.	17	Director responsible—1 Students responsible—2
e) The Business Manager should give bond for the protection of the band, and for the return of instruments, uniforms, and equipment. This bond should not be less than $1000.00 and should be handled through the band budget.	9	?—3 Yes, unless handled by military officer—2 Director responsible—1 No—1 Each member responsible—4
4. LIBRARIAN a) The Librarian should index and file all music, under the direction of the Director.	18	Director and Custodian—2
b) The Librarian should make up march books and concert folios as needed with the help of other band men.	18	Director and Custodian—2
c. The Librarian should have complete charge of all band music.	18	Director and Custodian—2
5. FIRST CHAIR MAN ON EACH SECTION a) The First Chair Man should help others in his section who need help.	18	Private lessons for small fee—1 Outside, but not during rehearsals—1

TABLE I—*Continued*

Tentative Standards	Answers to Tentative Standards	
	Agree	Other Opinions
5. FIRST CHAIR MAN ON EACH SECTION—*Cont'd.* *b)* The First Chair Man should hold section rehearsals for his section as needed.	16	With help and advice of Director—1 If experienced and upper classman—1 Director should hold them—2
c) The First Chair Man should help the Director place the men on parts in his section.	13	Why—2 Not necessary—1 Whole band at tryouts—1 Yes, Director power to determine—2 If experienced and upper classman—1
6. DRUM MAJOR *a)* The Drum Major should have complete charge of the band at all times when on parade.	18	Yes, Director or Assistant indicates music—2
IV. No student officer of the band should be paid for his services.	13	Better officers if paid—2 Librarian should be paid—1 Assistant Director paid—1 If enough duties pay them—1 Pay band Custodian—1 ?—1
B. EQUIPMENT I. The larger instruments and those not usually purchased by students should be furnished by the Institution free of charge.	13	University and War Dept.—1 Or by Band Budget—1 Bass drum and cymbals, others if interest lacking—2
II. Larger instruments and those not usually purchased by students should be rented to students at a nominal fee, at least large enough to cover annual repairs on set rented.	3	
III. Students should be required to place a deposit of not less than $10.00 on instruments furnished free by the college and issued to them.	12	No—1 Students responsible for damage—3 Yes, deposit not returnable—1
IV. Uniforms should be furnished free to members of the band.	18	
V. Uniforms should be rented to students at a nominal fee, at least large enough to cover cleaning and repair of the uniform for the year.		Students should pay for cleaning—2 Students should buy uniforms—1 ?—2 Fee large enough to buy new suit when worn out—1 No—14
VI. A deposit of not less than $5.00 should be made by each student on the uniform issued to him, where the uniforms are furnished free by the college.	13	Why?—3 Students held responsible—3 No—1

TABLE I—*Continued*

TENTATIVE STANDARDS	Answers to Tentative Standards	
	Agree	Other Opinions
B. EQUIPMENT—*Continued* VII. A deposit of not less than 50c should be made by each student for each march book issued to him.	10	Student responsible for all music—4 Flat band fee best—1 ?—2 No—3
C. ACTIVITIES I. There should be at least 120 minutes per week spent in actual rehearsal; more time is necessary for the best results.	18	Daily during school hrs. best—1 Not enough time—1
II. The functions at which the bands play should be limited to: 1. The Concert Band should handle those functions at which a band may secure the best musical results. Athletic contests, except the big games of the year, marching, parades, reviews, etc., should be left for the Military Band.	17	Big games combined bands—1 ?—1 Yes, if there is one—1
2. The Military Band should be used for military reviews, marching, most of the athletic contests, and outside work, with the exception of spring open air concerts.	19	?—1
III. Concert trips, where possible should be arranged for the Concert Band in order to increase interest and furnish an incentive for careful musical work and the development of well rounded programs.	20	
IV. Free open air concerts by the Concert Band, or a combination of bands, should be given in the spring as soon as the weather permits.	18	A limited number—1 Yes, must work with A. F. of M. —1
V. Where possible, an Honorary Society or Fraternity should be sponsored to add incentive for service beyond the Military Band.	17	Too many already—1 ?—1 If they are allowed—1
D. FINANCING I. All financial matters should be handled through the Bursar's or Treasurer's office.	19	Too much red tape—1
II. A regular budget should be provided in which provision is made for: 1. The purchase of new instruments as needed by the band.	20	
2. The repair of instruments owned by the college or university.	20	

TABLE I—*Continued*

Tentative Standards	Answers to Tentative Standards	
	Agree	Other Opinions
D. Financing—*Continued* 3. The purchase of new music as needed for the band. A minimum of $50.00 annually for each multiple of 25 men in band work is a reasonable standard.	17	No minimum—1 Minimum too low—2
4. The replacement of old instruments at regular periods.	20	
5. The purchase and replacement of uniforms as needed.	20	
6. The depreciation to charge off on band instruments owned by the college.	19	Instruments and Music—1
7. The depreciation to charge off on uniforms owned by the college.	20	
8. The bond of the Business Manager of the band.	14	If bond is given—1 ?—1, No—3, Have none—1
Note—The following questions have to do with the matter of credit being allowed for band work over and above that given for military drill.		
E. College Credit I. College credit *should not* be allowed for band work over and above that given for military drill.	3	
II. College credit *should be allowed* for band work over and above that given for military drill.	16	For Juniors and Seniors
III. College credit should be allowed for band work: 1. As a free elective on all courses of the college or university.	17	
2. As a free elective on Music and Arts courses offered by the college or university.	3	
IV. College credit should be allowed for band work on the basis of: 1. Time put in at rehearsals or other regular scheduled work of the band which may be called educational.	19	When individual instruction is given—1
2. Improvement of the men during the year on their respective instruments.	14	Yes, grades rather than credit—2 When individual instruction given—1
3. The original ability of the men and their usefulness to the band.	6	Should be considered—3 When individual instruction given—1

TABLE I—*Continued*

TENTATIVE STANDARDS	Answers to Tentative Standards	
	Agree	Other Opinions
E. COLLEGE CREDIT—*Continued* 4. A combination of the above ((1), (2), (3)). State what combination is best.		(1) and (2)—7 (1)—1 (2)—1 (1), (2), and (3)—5 (1) and (2)—1 (1), (2), (3) + attitude and responsibility—1
5. Other possibilities as a basis for giving credit. State any that seem good to you.		Faithfulness and loyalty—1 (above) Willingness to work and aid band, proper interest—1 (given above) Study of classics in music—1 Interpretive ability, theoretical and esthetic musical knowledge—1

masters voting for the standard as indicated in the survey blank. Where the tentative standard was not satisfactory, a brief statement was made indicating what would be considered a satisfactory standard.

I. For example, under "The Director of the Band should be a member of the Music Department of the Institution"—18 voted for this statement as a standard while 2 indicated that he need "not necessarily" be a member of the music department of the institution. Since 18 of the bandmasters checked the standard indicating that the director of the band should be a member of the music department of the institution, we may reasonably take this as one of the standards.

II. "The duties of the officers of the band should be clearly stated in the Constitution and By-Laws of the band."—We find that 17 voted for the statement as indicated; 2 of the bandmasters said that these duties should be stated in the constitution and by-laws or R.O.T.C. regulations; and 1 indicated that the constitution and by-laws are unnecessary. We may assume from this that 95 per cent of the bandmasters feel that duties of officers should be clearly stated either in the constitution and by-laws of the band or in R.O.T.C. regulations.

III. Duties of Officers
1. *Director*
   a) "The Director should have direct charge of the band at all functions at which the band plays."—

17 voted for this standard; 2 said that the director should not be required to attend· all student functions; and 1 said that the student director should have direct charge of the band. As the band always does much better under the regular director than under the student director, this standard should be closely observed except in case of illness or other emergency.

b) The Director should make requisitions through the Bursar for:

(1) "The purchase of new music."—17 voted for the standard as stated; 1 indicated that the director should make requisition through the budget for instruments and music; 1 indicated the approval of the head of the music department as essential; and 1 stated that purchase should be made through the purchasing department. We could assume from this that the director should make requisition through the bursar's office or purchasing department for the purchase of new music and, in case the director is working under the head of the music department, the approval of the latter should be secured.

(2) "The purchase of new instruments and supplies for the band."—We have again 17 voting for the standard as indicated, 2 stating that the requisition should go through the director of music, and 1 that it should go through the purchasing department. In any case the requisition is placed through the regular business channels of the institution.

(3) "The repair of instruments and equipment as needed."—17 voted for the standard as indicated; 1 said that the director should O.K. the requisition; 1 that the head of the music department should do so; and 1 indicated that the requisition should go through the purchasing department rather than the bursar. This would also indicate a strong sentiment

that the finances of the band should be handled through the regular business offices of the institution.

(4) "The replacement of instruments and equipment which are worn out."—18 voted for this statement as a standard, 1 indicating that the approval of the head of the music department was necessary, and 1 favoring the purchasing department. These responses would indicate that the statement as made is a satisfactory standard.

(5) "The purchase, replacement, and repair of uniforms as needed."—16 voted for the statement as given; 1 indicated that the approval of the head of the music department should be secured; 2 said that this should be a function of the director unless handled through the military department or R.O.T.C.; while 1 questioned the statement without criticism. It may be assumed that this is a reasonable standard, since a band organized under the R.O.T.C. regulations would naturally be handled through the regular army channels.

c) "The Director should coöperate with the Business Manager in making business arrangements for all appearances of the band. The Director should be responsible for these in the final analysis."—16 voted for the statement as made; 2 indicated that the director should be in an advisory capacity; 1 said if the manager was a band member, "Yes," but in case the business manager was a faculty member, "No"; 1 questioned the statement without giving any criticism. Since it is implied that the director should be in an advisory capacity, we may say that 18 voted for the statement as indicated, which would show that it is a reasonable standard.

d) "The Director should give instruction on band instruments through the Music Department."—10 voted for the statement as submitted; 4 said, "Not necessarily"; 1 indicated that if the director had time he should give instruction through the music department; 3 stated that the director should give instruction on band instruments through the music department or make arrangements for competent instruction; 2 said that in case there was a music department, instruction should be given as indicated. Combining these we might say that we have 16 voting for the standard while 4 indicate, "Not necessarily." From this we may assume that where there is a music department in the institution and where the director gives instruction on band instruments for a fee, these lessons should be given through the music department. Private lessons given through the music department are often prohibitive in price to many of the students who wish instruction. For this reason instrumental classes should supplement private instruction, similar to the movement which has developed in public schools. This would reduce the cost of instruction and make it available to a large number of students at a nominal fee.

In a college or university band organization, the director is responsible for all band activities and the functioning of the band. Many of these duties should be delegated, however, to student officers. In this way, students in the band would be trained for future organization and activity work connected with public school or community bands. The following list of student officers was made up from the 54 college and university bands returning the original survey blanks. Where the band was organized as a R.O.T.C. unit, the names of officers of the band varied in a few cases, but their duties remained essentially the same. The duties of student officers of the band, therefore, covered rather the functions to be performed by the various officers even though the definite duties as indicated may be handled by some other student officer of the band.

2. *Student Director*

    a) "The Student Director should be in direct charge of the band in the absence of the Director."—18 voted for the statement as indicated; 1 said the student director or R.O.T.C. officer should be in charge in the absence of the director; and 1 indicated that the student director or assistant director should be a regular member of the music department. This would indicate that the student director or assistant director should be next in charge under the director.

    b) "The Student Director should arrange for section rehearsals."—13 voted for the statement as submitted, while 7 indicated that the student director should arrange for section rehearsals under the director's guidance. In view of the fact that these student officers are working under the director at all times, it may be assumed that the student director would not arrange for section rehearsals without the guidance of the director.

    c) "The Student Director should take the roll of the band at rehearsals and at all functions where the band plays."—11 voted for the statement as given; 4 stated that the student director or secretary should take the roll; 3 indicated that the sergeant or secretary should take the roll; and 2 indicated the taking of the roll as a function of the drum major. This function of the student director may be influenced by other duties which are assigned to him; however, when we accept as a standard that the director should have direct charge of the band at all functions at which the band plays, this should leave the student director free to take the roll while the director tunes the band, arranges the music, etc.

    d) "The Student Director should assist the Director at all times."—19 voted for this statement as a standard while 1 voted for the statement but indicated that the assistant director should be a regular member of the music department.

3. *Business Manager*

    a) "The Business Manager should arrange for the transportation of men and instruments at all functions at which the band plays."—19 voted for the standard as given, while 1 indicated that this should be a function of the captain of the band. We may assume that this is rightfully a function and duty of the business manager in the majority of bands.

    b) "The Business Manager should have charge of the instruments and uniforms, checking them in and out to the band members as needed."—14 voted for the standard as submitted; 2 indicated that the business manager should have charge of the instruments and uniforms unless this work was handled through a military officer; 2 indicated that the director should oversee it; and 2 stated that this was a duty of the custodians of the band. On this point we have a difference in title of officers appearing particularly in bands organized under R.O.T.C. regulations. If we combine those voting for custodians, those indicating it as a duty unless handled by a military officer, and the 14 voting for the standard as submitted, we have a total of 18 out of 20. In most bands this is a definite function of the business manager or other officer carrying on the same group of functions, and perhaps should remain so.

    c) "The Business Manager should make arrangements for the Spring Tour with the help of the Director and Bursar."—17 agreed that this should be a standard while 1 said the business manager should arrange for any tour, 1 indicated that the business manager should handle business arrangements for the spring tour if one was taken, and 1 indicated that the captain and seniors should make arrangements for the tour. We may say that 19 out of 20 voted for this standard.

    d) "The Business Manager should be responsible for all band equipment, under the Director."—17 voted for the tentative standard as stated; 1 indicated that the director was responsible; and 2 indicated that the students should be responsible. In regard to this point it seems only fair that the students should be responsible for the care and condition of all band equipment, but that the business manager should be directly responsible for the issuing and care of equipment during the time that the equipment is not in use. He should also be responsible for the return of all equipment issued.

e) "The Business Manager should give bond, for the protection of the band, for the return of instruments, uniforms, and equipment. This bond should not be less than $1,000 and should be handled through the band budget."—9 voted for the standard as submitted; 2 said that the business manager should give bond unless this duty was handled by a military officer; 4 indicated that each member of the band should be responsible; 1 stated that the director was responsible; 3 questioned the statement without comment; and 1 indicated that the business manager should not give bond. On this point again it would seem that each member should be responsible for damage to instruments, uniforms, and equipment, aside from ordinary wear, but that the business manager should be very definitely responsible to the band for a careful check on all instruments, uniforms, and equipment at any time. This bond of $1,000 would be required not so much for protection in case of loss, but as a guaranty of careful methods of checking of all uniforms, instruments, and equipment when issued and returned. The band members would be more careful in returning equipment, if they knew that the business manager was under bond for all instruments, uniforms, and equipment owned by the band or college. Where the bond is given by the business manager he should be the only one to handle instruments, uniforms, and equipment. The equipment of college and university bands represents an investment ranging from a few thousand to as high as twenty-five thousand dollars. Provision must be made for the careful handling of all equipment entrusted to the business manager. This is particularly true when the instruments and equipment are checked back at the end of the school year. Student officers are often careless at this time because of examinations and the general press of other college duties.

4. *Librarian*

   a) "The Librarian should index and file all music, under the direction of the Director."—18 voted for this as one of the functions of the librarian, while 2 indicated that the director and custodian should index and file all music. Since this duty is largely clerical, the director should be relieved of the responsibility by the librarian. It would seem that this is one of the definite duties that a librarian should perform.

   b) "The Librarian should make up march books and concert folios as needed, with the help of other bandmen." Again we find that 18 voted for this as one of the duties of a librarian, while the same 2 as under (a) indicated that the director and custodian should handle the march books and concert folios. Here again the director should indicate the arrangement of numbers but should be relieved of the clerical work involved.

   c) "The Librarian should have complete charge of all band music."—18 accepted this as a duty of the librarian with 2 indicating that the director and custodian should have complete charge of all band music. The custodian, as indicated in this point, is usually assigned this function of the librarian.

5. *First Chair Man on Each Section*

   a) "The First Chair Man should help others in his section who need help."—18 voted for this as a function of the first chair man of each section; 1 indicated that the first chair man should give private lessons for a small fee; and 1 said that help should be given but not during rehearsals.

   b) "The First Chair Man should hold section rehearsals for his section as needed."—16 voted for this as one of the functions of the first chair man; 1 indicated that the first chair man should handle it with the help and advice of the director; 1 said that if he was experienced and an upper-classman he should handle it; and 2 indicated that the director should hold section rehearsals. Again this seems like a reasonable function of the first chair man. Where class instrumental instruction is provided at a nominal fee, the section rehearsals conducted by the first chair man would supplement such training.

c) "The First Chair Man should help the Director place the men on parts in his section."—13 voted for this standard as stated; 1 indicated that his help was not necessary; 1 said that the whole band at tryouts should be used in placing the men on parts; 2 indicated that the first chair man should help the director but the director should have the power to determine which place the man would receive; 1 stated that the first chair man, where experienced and an upper-classman, should perform this function; and 2 asked the question, "Why?" without any comment. Combining these we have 16 that would vote for the main idea incorporated in this point. The first chair man is in a position to be of great help. He can check the playing ability oftentimes even better than the director, and, in cases where he is capable, his experience and ability should be used and developed. This method stimulates leadership and interest through the key men of each section.

6. *Drum Major*

a) "The Drum Major should have complete charge of the band at all times when on parade."—18 voted for the standard as submitted; 2 said that the drum major should have complete charge of the band but that the director or assistant should indicate the music to be played. The designation of music may be left to the leader or student director since the drum major frequently is not a musician. In all other matters he should be in complete charge of the band.

IV. "No Student Officer of the band should be paid for his services."—13 voted for this statement; 2 indicated that better officers would be secured if they were paid; 1 said that the librarians should be paid; 1 indicated that the assistant director should be paid; 1 said that if the student officer had enough duties he should be paid; 1 stated that the band custodian should be paid; and 1 questioned the statement without comment. It is reasonable to assume that where the student officers have duties as indicated they should not be paid for their services. Where several of the officers and their functions are combined there might be some legitimate reason for paying them for their services. On the whole, however, the functions of a student officer should be looked on as educational for the person holding the office and for that reason he should not be paid for his services. The function of student officers should be looked on as a privilege and opportunity for training in band work. Student officers of other college curricular and extra-curricular activities are seldom paid for their services, and, in general, this rule should apply to band work.

B. EQUIPMENT

I. "The larger instruments and those not usually purchased by students should be furnished by the Institution free of charge."—13 voted for this as a standard for college and university bands, 1 indicated that the university and War Department should handle the larger instruments, 1 stated that they should be handled through the band budget or by the institution, 2 said that the bass drum and cymbals and other instruments, where interest was lacking, should be furnished free of charge. Combining these, we find that 17 voted for the statement as a standard and for the handling of the larger instruments in some way through the institution. Those instruments listed in Table V A should be furnished free of charge by the institution when this point is accepted as a standard.

II. "Larger instruments and those not usually purchased by students should be rented to students at a nominal fee, at least large enough to cover annual repairs on the set rented."—Only 3 indicated that larger instruments and those not usually purchased by students should be rented by them.

III. "Students should be required to place a deposit of not less than $10 on instruments furnished free by the college and issued to them."—12 voted for this statement as a standard, 3 indicated that students should be responsible for damage, 1 indicated that the students should make a deposit of $10 which would not be returnable, and 1 said that no deposit should be required. When instruments are furnished free by the institution it is only reasonable to accept a deposit on the instrument, not to cover damage but to insure its safe return. Students should in all cases be responsible for damage. A careful check should be made on the condition of each instrument before it is issued and when it is returned, in order to determine damage or injury during the time it was in use.

IV. "Uniforms should be furnished free to members of the band."—18 indicated that uniforms should be furnished free to members of the band. Where tuxedos or other parts of the uniform are used for other than band functions, the college may be justified in asking the students to furnish these items.

V. "Uniforms should be rented to students at a nominal fee, at least large enough to cover cleaning and repair of the uniform for the year."—1 indicated that students should buy their uniforms, 1 that the rental should be large enough to buy a new uniform when the old one was worn out; 2 stated that the students should pay for cleaning; 2 questioned the statement without comment, and 14 indicated that uniforms should not be rented to students. This would indicate that only 1 feels that the students should furnish their uniforms and 1 that the uniforms should be rented to students.

VI. "A deposit of not less than $5.00 should be made by each student on the uniform issued to him, where the uniforms are furnished free by the college."—13 voted for a deposit being placed on the uniform issued to the student; 3 indicated that the student should be responsible for the uniform; 3 asked the question, "Why?" without comment; and 1 definitely said, "No." Here, as under sub-topic III, we have the question of a small deposit being placed on equipment to insure its return. In case of unusual damage a more satisfactory adjustment can be worked out than would be possible were the student required to make good the damage without having placed a deposit on the equipment. In the issuing of uniforms, as in the issuing of instruments, a careful check should be made of the condition of each article when it is issued and again when it is turned in. In case of damage, the amount required to place the uniform in condition may be deducted from the deposit fee. Where the business manager is required to give bond for careful handling of equipment and a deposit is required on instruments and uniforms, the careful handling of all band property is assured.

VII. "A deposit of not less than 50¢ should be made by each student for each march book issued to him."—10 indicated that a deposit should be made on each march book issued; 4 said that the student should be responsible for all music issued to him; 1 indicated that a flat band fee was best; 2 questioned the advisability of requiring a 50¢ deposit; while 3 definitely said, "No." We again have the question of a deposit being required on equipment owned by the band and issued to a band member. This 50¢ deposit would not cover the cost of making up a march book but it would be an inducement for a band member to turn in his book at the end of the year. Without a deposit many books are lost, due to indifference or negligence on the part of members of the band.

C. ACTIVITIES

I. "There should be at least 120 minutes per week spent in actual rehearsal; more time is necessary for the best results."—18 indicated that at least 120 minutes per week should be spent in actual rehearsal, 1 indicated that this was not enough time, and 1 suggested that daily rehearsal during school hours is best, with a total of at least 250 minutes. 120 minutes per week spent in actual rehearsal should be the minimum standard for each band.

II. "The functions at which the bands play should be limited:
  1. The concert band should handle those functions at which a band may secure the best musical results. Athletic contests, except the big games of the year, marching, parades, reviews, etc., should be left to the military band."—17 voted for this statement of the function of the concert band; 1 indicated that combined bands should be used at the big games of the year; 1 said that this differentiation in function of the concert band should be made in case the institution had a concert band; and 1 questioned the differentiation of function. We may say, then, that 19 voted for the standard as stated.
  2. "The military band should be used for military reviews, marching, most of the athletic contests, and outside work, with the exception of spring open air concerts."—19 voted for this statement of the function of the military band and 1 questioned the statement without comment.

III. "Concert trips, where possible, should be arranged for the concert band in order to increase interest and furnish an incentive for careful musical work and the development of well-rounded programs."—20, or the entire group, indicated that concert trips where possible should be arranged for the concert band.

IV. "Free open air concerts by the concert band, or a combination of bands, should be given in the spring as soon as the weather permits."—18 voted for free open air concerts; 1 indicated that a limited number should be given each year; and 1 stated that they should be given but that the college or university band must work in coöperation with the A. F. of M.

V. "Where possible, an honorary society or fraternity should be sponsored to add incentive for service beyond the military band."—17 indicated that an honor society or fraternity should be sponsored; 1 said that it should be sponsored in case it was allowed at the institution; 1 questioned the advisability of fostering an honor society or fraternity, and 1 indicated that there were too many already. Where an honorary society or fraternity has been organized in connection with band work, it has proved a great incentive particularly among the juniors and seniors. Many of the devices used by bands, as shown in Table X, will be included in the activities of such an organization or will be found unnecessary.

D. FINANCING

I. "All financial matters should be handled through the bursar's or treasurer's office."—19 indicated that all financial matters should be handled through the bursar's or treasurer's office, while 1 thought that this involved too much red tape. Since the bursar's office is equipped to handle matters of finance and budget, requisitions on the annual band budget may be taken care of as easily through this department as through the department of music.

II. "A regular budget should be provided in which provision is made for:

1. The purchase of new instruments as needed by the band."—20, or the entire group, voted for this as a standard for bands.

2. "The repair of instruments owned by the college or university."—Again we find that the entire group, or 20, voted for this statement as a standard. The total annual amount needed for repairs, outside of damage, may be accurately determined by using Table XVII in the Appendix.

3. "The purchase of new music as needed for the band. A minimum of $50.00 annually for each multiple of 25 men in band work is a reasonable standard."—17 voted for this phase of the tentative standard; 1 indicated that there should be no minimum; while 2 indicated that the minimum was too low.

4. "The replacement of old instruments at regular periods."—The entire group, or 20, voted for this point as a standard. The length of life of the various band instruments may be determined from a study of Table XVII and the budget made out to include replacements when needed.

5. "The purchase and replacement of uniforms as needed."
   —Again we have the entire group, or 20, voting for this
   feature of the budget. The replacement of the uniforms may be accurately determined ahead by consulting the figures given in Table XVIII.
6. "The depreciation to charge off on band instruments
   owned by the college."—19 voted for the statement as
   indicated, while 1 said that the budget should show
   depreciation to charge off on band instruments and
   music. Depreciation may be determined by consulting
   Table XVII.
7. "The depreciation to charge off on uniforms owned by
   the college."—20 voted for this statement as a part of
   the budget. Depreciation on uniforms may be easily
   determined from a study of Table XVIII.
8. "The bond of the Business Manager of the band."—14
   indicated that the bond of the business manager should
   be placed in the band budget; 1 stated that it should
   be placed in the budget if a bond was to be given; 3
   answered "No"; 1 indicated that there was no business
   manager in their band; and 1 questioned the statement
   without comment. If we hold as a standard that the
   business manager of the band should be placed under
   bond for the handling of band instruments, uniforms,
   and equipment, this bond should be furnished by the
   band and should appear in the regular band budget.

E. College Credit

On the question as to whether credit should be allowed for
band work over and above that given for military drill, 17 felt
that credit should be allowed, while 3 replied that it was not
necessary.

In considering the question of college credit being allowed for
band work as (1) a free elective on all courses of the college
or university, or (2) a free elective on music and arts courses
offered by the college or university, we find that 17 stated that
it should be a free elective on all courses of the college or university, while 3 indicated that credit should be allowed on
music and arts courses only.

TABLE II

FUNCTIONS OF COLLEGE BANDS

(The functions of college bands at various activities were checked by eighteen of the twenty bandmasters responding.)

ACTIVITIES AT WHICH THE COLLEGE BANDS PLAYED	Chief Functions of College Bands at Various Activities, as Checked by Twenty Bandmasters					
	Mainly Public-ity	Mainly Extra-Curric-ular	Mainly Educa-tional	Mainly Remu-nerative	Mainly Serv-ice to College	Divided between Several
1. Football Games............	9	7			1	1
2. Basketball Games.........	9	7			1	1
3. Wrestling Meets..........	7	9			1	1
4. Track Meets..............	8	8			1	1
5. Baseball Games...........	8	8			1	1
6. Pep Meetings.............	7	10				1
7. Pep Parades Before and After Games............	9	8				1
8. Political Meetings on the Campus................	5	8		3	1	1
9. Convocations and Assemblies................	4	7	6		1	
10. Graduation Exercises......	6	7	3	1	1	
11. Spring Open Air Concerts	4	4	8		1	1
12. Special Concerts with Paid Admission..............	1	1	3	10		3
13. Dedication Exercises, All Kinds.................	10	4	2	1	1	
14. Carnivals, Campfires, Picnics, etc. Conducted by the College.............	6	11			1	
15. Receptions...............	8	7		2	1	
16. Dinners, on and off the Campus................	7	7		2	1	1
17. Spring Tours of the Band..	7	1	4	3		3
18. Radio Broadcasting by the Band..................	12	1	1			4
19. Playing at County or State Fairs..................	3		2	10		3
20. Regular Rehearsals of the Band..................		1	16			1
21. Special Rehearsals in Preparation for Spring Tours, Concerts, etc...........		3	14			1

NOTE—The above list includes all of the activities at which the 54 bands, included in the study, played last year.

Approaching the problem from a different angle, we find that 19 of the bandmasters voted that college credit be allowed for band work on the basis of time put in at rehearsals or for regular scheduled work of the band which may be called educational, and 1 bandmaster voted for this standard when individual instruction was given.

Replies from 16 of the bandmasters indicated that credit should be allowed on the basis of the improvement of the men during the year on their respective instruments. One stated that it should be considered when individual instruction was given. This might be determined by written and playing tests as a basis for careful, accurate grading in keeping with the college academic standards.[1] Where class or private instruction is taken by the student, this may replace the written or playing tests in determining improvement.

Considering as a basis for credit the original ability of the men and their usefulness to the band, 6 indicated that this was a desirable method to employ, 3 felt that it should be considered, and 1 said that when individual instruction was given it should be included. This is not conclusive enough to set up a standard.

The activities at which college bands play may roughly be grouped into four divisions: "mainly publicity," "mainly extra-curricular," "mainly educational," and "mainly remunerative." Of these four divisions we are justified in allowing college credit on those activities which are mainly educational. Table II shows that in the list of activities as checked by 18 of the 20 bandmasters, 16, or 88.9 per cent, checked rehearsals as mainly educational; 1, as extra-curricular; and 1 divided rehearsals between extra-curricular activities and activities that are mainly educational. We find also that 14, or 77.8 per cent, indicated that special rehearsals were mainly educational. These are the only two activities on which there seemed to be any agreement as to educational value.

Public school bands are coming to four considerations for the giving of credit:

(1) A regular lesson must be taken by the band member each week during the school year.

---

[1] James, Lynn L., "Raising Musicians Out Where the West Begins." *Jacobs Band Monthly*, April 1926.

(2) He must attend all weekly rehearsals.

(3) He must practice a specified amount each week.

(4) When requested he must play at any entertainment sponsored by the school authorities.[2]

In place of considering the original ability of the men and their usefulness to the band as a basis for credit, we could substitute as a standard that, when requested, the members of the college band should play at any activity agreed on by a majority of the band members.

"Now a high school student may be certain of acceptance in a good college somewhere, even if his music work approaches one-third of his high school training." [3]

In a study made by Osbourne McConathy,[4] it was found that out of 419 colleges and universities coöperating, 247 allowed some credit in music toward the academic degree, 87 allowed more than 20 semester hours in music, and 112 allowed credit in applied music toward the degree.

Thirteen of the bandmasters located at institutions where college credit is not allowed for band work indicated on the original survey that college credit would greatly help in the future improvement of their respective bands. In light of the above conditions it would seem reasonable to give college credit for band work on the basis (a) of time spent at rehearsal, (b) of improvement of the men on their respective instruments during the year as determined by written or playing tests or by private or group lessons pursued throughout the year under the music department, and (c) of playing at all activities voted on and approved by the band.

The amount of credit to be given for band work should be based on the time spent at rehearsal, since it is primarily educational. Two hours per week spent at rehearsal for 18 weeks should receive one semester hour of credit. This would mean that from four to eight semester hours of credit could be earned in band work depending on whether or not it may be substituted for military drill. Where a military department does not exist,

[2] Maddy, J. E., *Instrumental Technique for Orchestra and Band.* Willis Music Company, Cincinnati, Ohio, 1926.

[3] Lockhart, Lee M., "College Entrance Requirements and Public School Music," *Jacobs Band Monthly,* October 1925.

[4] *Present Status of Music Instruction in Colleges and High Schools,* 1919-1920. Bureau of Education, Washington, D. C., 1921. 54 pp.

the student could earn eight semester hours' credit as a free elective.

If credit is allowed for private or class instrumental lessons, this should be handled through the music department. Where a music department does not exist, no credit should be allowed for such lessons, as they will not then be handled through a regular department of the college.

CHAPTER III

COLLEGES, UNIVERSITIES, AND NORMAL SCHOOLS AND TEACHERS COLLEGES PROJECTED AGAINST THE STANDARDS SET UP FOR BANDS

The colleges, universities, and normal schools and teachers colleges that returned blanks covering the school year 1926-1927 are given below. An arbitrary division of these institutions into three groups has been made. The first group includes colleges and universities which are not organized on the R.O.T.C. or military basis primarily, although a few instruments or uniforms may be furnished by the army. The second group includes those colleges which are organized primarily on the R.O.T.C. basis or which receive a considerable amount of aid in uniforms or instruments for the army. Group three includes normal schools and teachers colleges. The following is the list of institutions included in the study, in the order in which they were recorded:

GROUP I

1. University of Chicago, Chicago, Illinois.
2. Brigham Young University, Provo, Utah.
3. Butler College, Indianapolis, Indiana.
4. University of California, Berkeley, California.
5. Carleton College, Northfield, Minnesota.
6. Carnegie Institute of Technology, Pittsburgh, Pennsylvania.
7. Columbia University, New York City.
8. Drake University, Des Moines, Iowa.
9. University of Iowa, Iowa City, Iowa.
10. Iowa Wesleyan College, Mt. Pleasant, Iowa.
11. University of Kentucky, Lexington, Kentucky.
12. Luther College, Decorah, Iowa.
13. University of Nevada, Reno, Nevada.
14. University of North Carolina, Chapel Hill, North Carolina.
15. Northwestern University, Evanston, Illinois.
16. Ohio Wesleyan University, Delaware, Ohio.
17. Oklahoma Agricultural and Mechanical College, Stillwater, Oklahoma
18. State University of South Carolina, Columbia, South Carolina.
19. University of Southern California, Los Angeles, California.
20. Stanford University, Palo Alto, California.

30

21. West Virginia Wesleyan College, Buckhannon, West Virginia.
22. University of Wisconsin, Madison, Wisconsin.
23. Wittenberg College, Springfield, Ohio.
24. Marquette University, Milwaukee, Wisconsin.
25. University of Michigan, Ann Arbor, Michigan.

GROUP II

26. Kansas State Agricultural College, Manhattan, Kansas.
27. University of Idaho, Moscow, Idaho.
28. Ohio State University, Columbus, Ohio.
29. University of South Dakota, Vermilion, South Dakota.
30. University of Wyoming, Laramie, Wyoming.
31. Mississippi Agricultural and Mechanical College, Agricultural College, Mississippi.
32. University of Nebraska, Lincoln, Nebraska.
33. University of Maine, Orono, Maine.
34. University of Arizona, Tucson, Arizona.
35. University of Arkansas, Fayetteville, Arkansas.
36. Colorado Agricultural College, Fort Collins, Colorado.
37. Iowa State College, Ames, Iowa.
38. North Carolina State College, Raleigh, North Carolina.
39. University of North Dakota, University, North Dakota.
40. North Dakota Agricultural College, Fargo, North Dakota.
41. University of Oklahoma, Norman, Oklahoma.
42. Oregon Agricultural College, Corvallis, Oregon.
43. Pennsylvania State College, State College, Pennsylvania.
44. University of Utah, Salt Lake City, Utah.

GROUP III

45. State Teachers College, Maryville, Missouri.
46. Northern State Normal School, Marquette, Michigan.
47. Kansas State Teachers College, Hays, Kansas.
48. Colorado State Teachers College, Greeley, Colorado.
49. Western Illinois State Teachers College, Macomb, Illinois.
50. Southern Illinois State Normal University, Carbondale, Illinois.
51. Indiana State Normal School, Muncie, Indiana. *Ball State or Indiana State*
52. Iowa State Teachers College, Cedar Falls, Iowa.
53. State Teachers College, Kearney, Nebraska.
54. Sam Houston State Teachers College, Huntsville, Texas.

The three groups of institutions as projected against the standards set up in Chapter II are tabulated in Table III.

A. PERSONNEL

I. "The Director of the band should be a member of the Music Department of the Institution." The three groups were projected against this standard with the following result:

Group I.................................. 20, or 80 per cent.
Group II................................. 13, or 68.4 per cent.
Group III................................ 9, or 90 per cent.

Considering the colleges as a whole, 42 out of 54, or 77.7 per cent, meet the standard.

II. "The duties of the officers of the band should be clearly stated in the Constitution and By-Laws of the band." In projecting the three groups against this standard, we have the following result:

Group I.................................. 18, or 72 per cent.
Group II................................. 14, or 73.6 per cent.
Group III................................ 7, or 70 per cent.

Considering all three groups, 39 out of 54, or 72.2 per cent, measure up to the standard.

III. Duties of Officers

1. *Director*

a) "The Director should have direct charge of the band at all functions at which the band plays." The three groups measure up to this standard as follows:

Group I.................................. 17, or 68 per cent.
Group II................................. 12, or 63.1 per cent.
Group III................................ 9, or 90 per cent.

Considering all three groups, 38 out of 54, or 70.3 per cent, come up to this standard.

b) "The Director should make requisitions through the Bursar for:

(1) The purchase of new music." The three groups were projected against this standard with the following result:

Group I.................................. 23, or 92 per cent.
Group II................................. 18, or 94.7 per cent.
Group III................................ 10, or 100 per cent.

Considering the three groups, 51 out of 54 bands, or a total of 94.4 per cent, meet this standard.

TABLE III

COLLEGES, UNIVERSITIES, AND NORMAL SCHOOLS AND TEACHERS COLLEGES
PROJECTED AGAINST THE STANDARDS SET UP FOR BANDS

(Group I—Colleges not R.O.T.C. Group II—Colleges R.O.T.C. Group III—Normal
Schools and Teachers Colleges)

STANDARDS	GROUP I	GROUP II	GROUP III	TOTAL
A. PERSONNEL I. The Director of the Band should be a member of the Music Department of the Institution.	20	13	9	42
II. The duties of the officers of the band should be clearly stated in the Constitution and By-Laws of the band.	18	14	7	39
III. The duties of the officers of the band should be as follows: 1. DIRECTOR a) The Director should have direct charge of the band at all functions at which the band plays.	17	12	9	38
b) The Director should make requisitions through the Bursar for: (1) The purchase of new music.	23	18	10	51
(2) The purchase of new instruments and supplies for the band.	21	16	10	47
(3) The repair of instruments and equipment as needed.	21	16	10	47
(4) The replacement of instruments and equipment which are worn out.	21	16	9	46
(5) The purchase, replacement, and repair of uniforms as needed.	20	16	9	45

TABLE III—*Continued*

STANDARDS	GROUP I	GROUP II	GROUP III	TOTAL
1. DIRECTOR—*Continued* *c)* The Director should cooperate with the Business Manager in making business arrangements for all appearances of the band. The Director should be responsible for these in the final analysis.	Dir 8 B.M. 10	Dir 8 B.M. 6	Dir 7	23 16
d) The Director should give instruction on band instruments through the Music Department.	12 Free 10	10 Free 9	8 Free 2	30 21
2. STUDENT DIRECTOR *a)* The Student Director should be in direct charge of the band in the absence of the Director.	20	14	8	42
b) The Student Director should arrange for section rehearsals.	5	3	3	11
c) The Student Director should take the roll of the band at rehearsals and at all functions where the band plays.	4	6	2	12
d) The Student Director should assist the Director at all times.	13	9	6	28
3. BUSINESS MANAGER *a)* The Business Manager should arrange for the transportation of men and instruments at all functions at which the band plays.	17	10		27
b) The Business Manager should have charge of the instruments and uniforms, checking them in and out to the band members as needed.	10	4		14

TABLE III—*Continued*

STANDARDS	GROUP I	GROUP II	GROUP III	TOTAL
3. BUSINESS MANAGER—*Cont'd.* c) The Business Manager should make arrangements for the Spring Tour with the help of the Director and Bursar.	12	5		17
d) The Business Manager should be responsible for all band equipment under the Director.	9	5		14
e) The Business Manager should give bond, for the protection of the band, for the return of instruments, uniforms, and equipment. This bond should not be less than $1000.00 and should be handled through the band budget.	0	0		0
4. LIBRARIAN a) The Librarian should index and file all music, under the direction of the Director.	16	9	2	27
b) The Librarian should make up march books and concert folios as needed, with the help of other bandmen.	14	7	2	23
c) The Librarian should have complete charge of all band music.	14	8	2	24
5. FIRST CHAIR MAN ON EACH SECTION a) The First Chair Man should help others in his section who need help.	11	10	1	22
b) The First Chair Man should hold section rehearsals for his section as needed.	9	6		15

TABLE III—*Continued*

Standards	GROUP I	GROUP II	GROUP III	TOTAL
5. FIRST CHAIR MAN ON EACH SECTION—*Continued* c) The First Chair Man should help the Director place the men on parts in his section.	6	7		13
6. DRUM MAJOR a) The Drum Major should have complete charge of the band at all times when on parade.	16	18	6	40
IV. No Student Officer of the band should be paid for his services.				
Do pay Student Director " " Business Manager " " Librarian	4 3 3	8 0 4	1 0 1	13 3 8
B. EQUIPMENT I. The larger instruments and those not usually purchased by students should be furnished by the Institution free of charge.	Tables IV and V	Tables IV and V	Tables IV and V	
II. Larger instruments and those not usually purchased by students should be rented to students at a nominal fee, at least large enough to cover annual repairs on the set rented.	Tables IV and V	Tables IV and V	Tables VI and V	
III. Students should be required to place a deposit of not less than $10.00 on instruments furnished free by the college and issued to them.				
IV. Uniforms should be furnished free to members of the band.	Table VI	Table VI	Table VI	
V. Uniforms should be rented to students at a nominal fee, at least large enough to cover cleaning and repair of the uniform for the year.	0	0	0	

TABLE III—*Continued*

STANDARDS	GROUP I	GROUP II	GROUP III	TOTAL
B. EQUIPMENT—*Continued*				
VI. A deposit of not less than $5.00 should be made by each student on the uniform issued to him, where the uniforms are furnished free by the college.				
VII. A deposit of not less than 50¢ should be made by each student for each march book issued to him.				
C. ACTIVITIES				
I. There should be at least 120 minutes per week spent in actual rehearsal; more time is necessary for the best results.	Table VII	Table VII	Table VII	
II. The functions at which the bands play should be limited to: 1. The Concert Band should handle those functions at which a band may secure the best musical results. Athletic contests, except the big games of the year, marching, parades, reviews, etc., should be left for the Military Band.	Tables VIII and IX	Tables VIII and IX	Tables VIII and IX	
2. The Military Band should be used for military reviews, marching, most of the athletic contests, and outside work, with the exception of spring open air concerts.	Tables VIII and IX	Tables VIII and IX	Tables VIII and IX	
III. Concert trips, where possible, should be arranged for the Concert Band in order to increase interest and furnish an incentive for careful musical work and the development of well rounded programs.	12	7	none	19

TABLE III—*Continued*

STANDARDS	GROUP I	GROUP II	GROUP III	TOTAL
C. ACTIVITIES—*Continued* IV. Free open air concerts by the Concert Band, or a combination of bands, should be given in the Spring as soon as the weather permits.	15	15	8	38
V. Where possible, an Honorary Society or Fraternity should be sponsored to add incentive for service beyond the military band.	Table X	Table X	Table X	
D. FINANCING I. All financial matters should be handled through the Bursar's or Treasurer's office.	15	7	2	24
II. A regular budget should be provided in which provision is made for: 1. The purchase of new instruments as needed by the band.	Table XI	Table XI	Table XI	
2. The repair of instruments owned by the college or university.	Table XII	Table XII	Table XII	
3. The purchase of new music as needed for the band. A minimum of $50.00 annually for each multiple of 25 men in band work is a reasonable standard.	Tables XIII and XIV	Tables XIII and XIV	Tables XIII and XIV	
4. The replacement of old instruments at regular periods.	Table XV	Table XV	Table XV	
5. The purchase and replacement of uniforms as needed.	Table XVI	Table XVI	Table XVI	
6. The depreciation to charge off on band instruments owned by the college.				

TABLE III—*Continued*

STANDARDS	GROUP I	GROUP II	GROUP III	TOTAL
D. FINANCING—*Continued* 7. The depreciation to charge off on uniforms owned by the college.				
8. The bond of the Business Manager of the band.				
III. College credit is allowed for band work: 1. As a free elective on all courses of the college or university.	9	7	3	19
2. As a free elective on Music and Arts courses offered by the college or university.	4	4	4	12

(2) In the purchase of new instruments and supplies for the band by requisition through the bursar's office, the three groups measure up to this standard as follows:

Group I.................................. 21, or 84 per cent.
Group II............................... 16, or 84.2 per cent.
Group III............................. 10, or 100 per cent.

Considering all three groups, 47 out of 54, or 87 per cent, meet the requirements of the standard.

(3) "The repair of instruments and equipment as needed." We have the following tabulation when the three groups are measured against this standard:

Group I.................................. 21, or 84 per cent.
Group II............................... 16, or 84.2 per cent.
Group III............................. 10, or 100 per cent.

Considering the three groups, a total of 47 out of 54, or 87 per cent, measure up to this standard.

(4) "The replacement of instruments and equipment which are worn out." The three groups were projected against this standard with the following result:

Group I.............................. 21, or 84 per cent.
Group II............................. 16, or 84.2 per cent.
Group III............................ 9, or 90 per cent.

Considering all three groups, a total of 48 out of 54, or 85.1 per cent, measure up to this standard of the duty of the director.

(5) "The purchase, replacement and repair of uniforms as needed." In considering this point, the three groups conform to the standard as follows:

Group I.............................. 20, or 80 per cent.
Group II............................. 16, or 84.2 per cent.
Group III............................ 9, or 90 per cent.

When all three groups are measured against the standard, we find that 45 out of 54, or 83.3 per cent, meet the requirement.

c) "The Director should coöperate with the Business Manager in making business arrangements for all appearances of the band. The Director should be responsible for these in the final analysis." In projecting the colleges against this standard we find that the function is performed in the various colleges by either the director or the business manager. In the three groups the function is performed by the director as follows:

Director:
Group I............................ 8, or 32 per cent.
Group II........................... 8, or 42.1 per cent.
Group III.......................... 7, or 70 per cent.

Considering all three groups, 23 out of 54, or 42.6 per cent, have the function performed by the director.

The business manager performs the function as follows:

Business Manager:

Group I........................... 10, or 40 per cent.
Group II.......................... 6, or 31.6 per cent.
Group III......................... 0

Considering the three groups, we find that 16, or 29.6 per cent, list this as a function of the business manager. Evidently, from our standard, there needs to be a clearer differentiation of function between the director and business manager in making business arrangements for all appearances of the band.

d) "The Director should give instruction on band instruments through the Music Department." In projecting the three groups against this standard, we find two ways in which instruction on band instruments is handled in the various colleges. A number of the instructors give lessons through the music department and many lessons are given free of charge by the director of the band in other institutions. In considering the group that give instruction on band instruments through the music department, we find that in

Group I.............. 12, or 48 per cent, give such instruction.
Group II............. 10, or 52.6 per cent, " " "
Group III............ 8, or 80 per cent, " " "

Considering all three groups, it appears that 30 out of 54, or 55.5 per cent, give instruction on band instruments through the music department. This figure is low, perhaps because of the fact that several of the colleges and universities considered do not have a music department organized for band instruction.

2. *Student Director*

a) "The Student Director should be in direct charge of the band in the absence of the Director." In considering this standard, we find that the three colleges appear as follows:

Group I............................... 20, or 80 per cent.
Group II.............................. 14, or 73.6 per cent.
Group III............................. 8, or 80 per cent.

Considering all three groups, we find that 42 out of 54, or 77.7 per cent, have this function performed by the student director or other student officer with the same group of duties.

b) "The Student Director should arrange for section rehearsals." The three groups were projected against this standard with the following result:

Group I............................... 5, or 20 per cent.
Group II.............................. 3, or 15.8 per cent.
Group III............................. 3, or 30 per cent.

Considering all of the institutions, we find that 11 out of 54, or 20.4 per cent, fulfill the requirements of this standard.

c) "The Student Director should take the roll of the band at rehearsals and at all functions where the band plays." The three groups as measured against this standard produce the following result:

Group I............................... 4, or 16 per cent.
Group II.............................. 6, or 31.6 per cent.
Group III............................. 2, or 20 per cent.

Considering all three groups, we find that 12 out of 54, or 22.2 per cent, meet the requirements of this standard.

d) "The Student Director should assist the Director at all times." In projecting the three groups against this standard, it is seen that they meet the requirements as follows:

Group I............................... 13, or 52 per cent.
Group II.............................. 9, or 47.3 per cent.
Group III............................. 6, or 60 per cent.

Considering all the institutions studied, we find that 28 out of 54, or 51.8 per cent, meet the standard requirements.

3. *Business Manager*

a) "The Business Manager should arrange for the transportation of men and instruments at all functions at which the band plays." We have the following tabulation from a projection of the three groups of colleges against this standard:

Group I................................ 17, or 68 per cent.
Group II............................... 10, or 52.6 per cent.
Group III.............................. 0

Considering the first and second groups, we have a total of 27 out of 54, or 50 per cent of the bands, that meet the requirements of this standard.

b) "The Business Manager should have charge of the instruments and uniforms, checking them in and out to the band members as needed." A tabulation of the colleges under this standard shows the following result:

Group I................................ 10, or 40 per cent.
Group II............................... 4, or 21 per cent.
Group III.............................. 0

This shows that 14 out of a possible 54, or 25.9 per cent of the bands, assign this duty to the business manager.

c) "The Business Manager should make arrangements for the Spring Tour with the help of the Director and Bursar." The three groups projected against this standard show the following result:

Group I................................ 12, or 48 per cent.
Group II............................... 5, or 26.3 per cent.
Group III.............................. 0

Out of the 54 bands under consideration, 17, or 31.5 per cent, indicate this function as belonging to the business manager.

d) "The Business Manager should be responsible for all band equipment, under the Director." The following indicates the status on this point of the three groups being considered:

Group I............................... 9, or 36 per cent.
Group II.............................. 5, or 26.3 per cent.
Group III............................. 0

This makes a total of 14 out of 54, or 25.9 per cent
of the bands included in the study.

e) "The Business Manager should give bond, for the
protection of the band, for the return of instruments, uniforms, and equipment. This bond should
not be less than $1,000 and should be handled
through the band budget." This point in the standard was formulated following the return of the
original survey blanks from the universities. The
returns indicated that some provision should be
made covering this item although no question was
asked on the original blank and hence no check can
be made.

4. *Librarian*

a) "The Librarian should index and file all music, under the direction of the Director." The three groups
were projected against this standard with the following result:

Group I............................... 16, or 64 per cent.
Group II.............................. 9, or 47.3 per cent.
Group III............................. 2, or 20 per cent.

This makes a total of 27 out of 54, or 50 per cent of
the bands that meet this standard.

b) "The Librarian should make up March Books and
Concert Folios as needed, with the help of other
band men." The tabulation below indicates the
status of the bands on this point:

Group I............................... 14, or 56 per cent.
Group II.............................. 7, or 36.8 per cent.
Group III............................. 2, or 20 per cent.

This makes a total of 23 out of a possible 54, or 46.6
per cent that meet this standard.

c) "The Librarian should have complete charge of all
band music." The groups were projected against
this standard with the following result:

Group I.................................. 14, or 56 per cent.
Group II................................. 8, or 42.1 per cent.
Group III............................... 2, or 20 per cent.

5. *First Chair Man on Each Section*
   a) "The First Chair Man should help others in his sec-
      tion who need help." This function of the first
      chair man may be summarized as follows:

Group I.................................. 11, or 44 per cent.
Group II................................. 10, or 52.6 per cent.
Group III............................... 1, or 10 per cent.

This shows that 22 out of 54, or 40.7 per cent, meet
this standard.
   b) "The First Chair Man should hold section rehearsals
      for his section as needed." The returns on this
      point are tabulated below:

Group I.................................. 9, or 36 per cent.
Group II................................. 6, or 31.6 per cent.
Group III......'........................... 0

This makes a total of 15 out of 54, or 27.8 per cent.
   c) "The First Chair Man should help the Director
      place the men on parts in his section." The colleges
      projected against this function show the following
      result:

Group I.................................. 6, or 24 per cent.
Group II................................. 7, or 36.8 per cent.
Group III............................... 0

This indicates that a total of 13 out of 54, or 24.1
per cent, meet this standard.
6. *Drum Major*
   a) "The Drum Major should have complete charge of
      the band at all times when on parade." A tabula-
      tion of this function of the drum major follows:

Group I.................................. 16, or 64 per cent.
Group II................................. 18, or 94.7 per cent.
Group III............................... 6, or 60 per cent.

TABLE IV

Band Instruments Used in College and University Bands

Kind of Instrument	Colleges not R.O.T.C. — Instruments Owned by Colleges, Free to Students	Colleges not R.O.T.C. — Owned by Colleges, Rented to Students	Colleges not R.O.T.C. — Instruments Furnished by Army	Colleges not R.O.T.C. — Instruments Owned by Students	Colleges R.O.T.C. — Owned by Colleges, Free to Students	Colleges R.O.T.C. — Owned by Colleges, Rented to Students	Colleges R.O.T.C. — Instruments Furnished by Army	Colleges R.O.T.C. — Instruments Owned by Students	Normal S. and T.C. — Owned by Colleges, Free to Students	Normal S. and T.C. — Owned by Colleges, Rented to Students	Normal S. and T.C. — Instruments Furnished by Army	Normal S. and T.C. — Instruments Owned by Students	Total
Piccolo	13	1	5	39	7		16	10	4	1		7	103
Flutes	8	5	7	44	4		27	17	7			12	131
Oboes	13	2	2	13	5	1	11	6	5			2	60
English Horns	3							2					5
Sarrusophones	5		1		1		3						10
Bassoons	13	3	2	4	7	2	11	2	4	1		2	51
E♭ Clarinets	13	5	5	8	6		14	2	3	1		2	59
B♭ Clarinets	50	28	26	299	20		148	163	18	3		58	813
Alto Clarinets	8	1	4	1			6	1					21
Bass Clarinets	9	1	4		1		8	2				1	26
C Soprano Saxophones		2		16	2		2	6				4	32
B♭ Soprano Saxophones	5	2	1	27			9	12	2			12	70
Alto Saxophones	5	3	3	75	4		22	61	2	1		18	194
C Melody Saxophones				42			2	24				8	76
B♭ Tenor Saxophones	10	2	3	37	3		21	25	3			8	112
E♭ Baritone Saxophones	10	2	2	12	5		16	7	3			3	60
B♭ Contra Bass Saxophones	3	1		2	3			3					12
French Horns	33	4	2	17	19		23	9	11	1		5	124

TABLE IV—*Continued*

Eb Altos—circular and upright..	69	14	9	33	34	2	43	19	21	5	6	255
Eb Cornets..	2	1							1	3		4
Bb Cornets..	26	14	5	154	5		43	53	7		23	333
Bb Trumpets..	20	8	6	181	6		50	133	7	4	36	447
Bb Tenor trombones—valve and slide..	35	18	8	163	10		54	80	12	2	31	415
Baritones—single and double bell	40	8	5	48	17		33	22	11	3	11	197
Eb Tubas, upright, helicon, sousaphone..	55	12	6	6	23		31	10	13	1	6	165
BBb Basses, upright, helicon, sousaphone..	38	4	9	24	10		33	9	2	2	3	133
Snare Drums..	67	14	3	29	18		37	20	12	2	8	210
Bass Drums..	32	4	5	5	17		21	3	9	2	1	99
Tympani..	24	2		2	20	3			11	1		64
String Basses..	23	2			23			1	14			64
Chimes and Marimbaphone..	2	1										3
Cello..	2				1		1					4
Bells..		1			1							4
Cymbals..	7				2		6					15
Flugel Horns..	5	1										6
Aida Trumpets..	3											3
Traps..	1	1		2								4
TOTAL..	654	165	123	1283	274	8	691	702	182	33	269	4384

Of the 54 bands we find that 40, or 74 per cent, meet this standard.

IV. "No Student Officer of the band should be paid for his services." The summary under this point is given according to the institutions which do pay certain student officers.

Group	Pay Student Director	Pay Business Manager	Pay Librarian
I.................	4	3	3
	16%	12%	12%
II................	8	....	4
	42.1%	....	21%
III...............	1	....	1
	10%	....	10%

B. Equipment

I and II. Table IV shows the total number of band instruments used in college and university bands. Below is a summary of this table:

Group	Instruments free to students	Instruments rented to students	Instruments furnished by Army	Instruments owned by students
I................	654	165	123	1283
	29.4%	7.4%	5.5%	57.7%
II..............	274	8	691	702
	16.3%	.6%	41.2%	41.9%
III.............	182	33	...	269
	37.6%	6.6%	...	55.8%

Table V shows the number of colleges in each group which make provision for the larger instruments and those not usually purchased by students. A summary of Table V is given in Table VA.

III. "Students should be required to place a deposit of not less than $10.00 on instruments furnished free by the college and issued to them." This standard seemed necessary from the replies to the original survey, but no question covering it was included in the original survey blank.

COLLEGES THAT FURNISH BAND INSTRUMENTS TO STUDENTS

Kind of Instrument	Number of Colleges without R.O.T.C. That Provide Instruments					Number of Colleges with R.O.T.C. That Provide Instruments				Number of Normal Schools and Teachers Colleges That Provide Instruments	
	Free to Students	Rented to Students	Free and Rented	Furnished by Army	Free and by Army	Free to Students	Rented to Students	Furnished by Army	Free and by Army	Free to Students	Rented to Students
Oboes	9	1			1	3	1	4	2	4	
English Horns	3				1	1		3		3	1
Sarrusophones	4	1			1	3		4	2	3	1
Bassoons	8	1		3	2	1	2	11	3		
Eb Clarinets	7	1		1	1			3			
Alto Clarinets	6	1		1	1			5			
Bass Clarinets	7			1	1	1		10	5	2	
Baritone Saxophones	7	2				2					
Bb Contra Bass Saxophones	3	1			1	5		5	2	5	1
French Horns	9	2			3	2	1	3	7	7	2
Eb Altos—circular and upright	15	1	1	2						7	2
Eb Cornets	2	1			1	2				8	1
Baritone—single and double bell	16	1	1	2	1	5		7	10	2	2
Eb Tubas—upright, helicon, sousaphone	17	1	1		3	1		6	8	8	2
BBb Basses, upright, helicon, sousaphone	11	2		1	4			9	8	8	
Snare Drums	17	1	1		2	2		6	11	5	1
Bass Drums	16	1	1	1	4	1		3	13	5	1
Tympani	11	1				10					
String Basses	11	1				10	1				
Chimes and Marimbaphone	2	1						1			
Cello	1					1					
Bells	2										
Cymbals	4										
Flugel Horns	2										

TABLE V A

INSTRUMENTS THAT SHOULD BE FURNISHED BY THE COLLEGE OR UNIVERSITY

KIND OF INSTRUMENT	Per Cent of the Colleges That Furnish at Least Part of These Instruments to Students		
	Group I	Group II	Group III
Oboes...	44	52.6	40
English Horns	12	0	0
Sarrusophones..................................	20	21.1	0
Bassoons..	40	57.9	40
E♭ Clarinets....................................	52	78.9	40
Alto Clarinets..................................	36	15.8	0
Bass Clarinets..................................	40	31.6	0
Baritone Saxophones...........................	44	78.9	20
B♭ Contra Bass Saxophones.....................	12	10.5	0
French Horns...................................	48	63.2	60
E♭ Altos—circular and upright.................	88	68.4	90
E♭ Cornets.....................................	12	0	10
Baritone—single and double bell.................	84	100	90
E♭ Tubas—upright, helicon, Sousaphone	88	100	100
BB♭ Basses " " "	72	94.7	30
Snare Drums....................................	84	94.7	100
Bass Drums.....................................	92	94.7	100
Tympani..	48	57.9	60
String Basses...................................	48	52.6	60
Chimes and Marimbaphone......................	12	0	0
Cello...	4	10.5	0
Bells...	8	0	0
Cymbals	16	0	0
Flugel Horns...................................	8	0	0

IV. and V. These points are covered in detail for each college in Table VI. A condensed summary stated in per cents appears:

Group	Uniforms furnished free to students	Uniforms furnished by Army	Uniforms furnished by students	Uniforms furnished by Athletic Association, etc.
I..............	50%	3.3%	18.7%	28%
II............	35.6%	34.6%	22.2%	7.6%
III...........	84.4%	...	15.6%	...

TABLE VI

FINANCING OF UNIFORMS USED BY COLLEGE AND UNIVERSITY BANDS

| College Number | Total Value of a Uniform | Part Furnished by College or University | | Part Furnished by Army | Part Furnished by Students | Part Furnished by Athletic Association, etc. | Number of Students with Complete Uniform |
		Free of Charge to Students	Rented to Students				
Group I.							
1...	$60.00		None			$60.00 Ath.	60
2...	16.00	$13.00	"		$3.00		49
3...	40.00	40.00	"				45
4...	50.00	50.00	"				96
	18.00			$18.00			60
5...	8.00	8.00	"				50
	35.00				35. (Tux)		40
6...	50.00					(Student Activity fee, Almuni, Ath. Assoc.) $50.00	50
7...	10.00	10.00	"				60
8...	27.25	4.95	"			(Collection at game and a play) $22.30	44
9 ..	5.00					(Popular subscription and Concerts) $5.00	65
10...	17.00	17.00					38
11...	30.00	Drum M.			30.00		60
12...	90.00					(Music Union) $90.00	60
13...	5.00	5.00					30
14...	15.00				15. 00		53
15...	30.00	30.00					83
16...	40.00						55
17...	15.00				15.00		130
18...	32.00	32.00					34
19...	25.00	8.00			17.00		150
20...	40.00	25.00			15.00		108
21...	No Uniform						
22...	40.00	10.00			30.00		162
23...	20.00	20.00					35
24	50.00	50.00					55
25...	43.00	43.00					72
Total...	$811.25	$405.95		$18.00	$160.00	$227.30	1,744

TABLE VI—*Continued*

College Number	Total Value of a Uniform	Part Furnished by College or University — Free of Charge to Students	Part Furnished by College or University — Rented to Students	Part Furnished by Army	Part Furnished by Students	Part Furnished by Athletic Association, etc.	Number of Students with Complete Uniform
Group II.							
26...	$35.00	$35.00	None				90
27...	16.50		"	$16.50			42
28...	50.00	15.00	"	35.00			100
29...	26.00		"		$26.00		36
30...	35.00			14.00		(Student Council) $21.00	35
31...	30.00				30.00		41
32...	30.00	30.00					98
33...	16.00			16.00			42
	35.00				35 (Tux)		61
34...	12.00			12.00			40
	12.00				12.00		39
35...	28.00			16.00	12.00		54
36...	35.00				35.00		34
37	40.00	40.00					80
38...	48.00			48.00			51
39...	16.00			16.00			70
	10.00	10.00					40
40...	39.00	5.00		34.00			75
41...	28.00			16.00	12.00		75
42...	44.50			13.50	10.00	(President gave cape) $21.00	52
43...	100.00	100.00					75
	23.00			23.00			135
44...	40.00	40.00					64
	23.00			23.00			38
Total..	$772.00	$275.00		$267.00	$172.00	$42.00	1,467
Group III.							
45...	$30.00				$30.00		35
46...	40.00	$35.00			5.00		50
47	15.00	15.00					50
48...	41.79	41.79					28
49...	12.00	12.00					20
50...	31.00	31.00					34
51...	48.00	48.00					35
52...	45.00	45.00					40
53...	25.00	22.00			3.00		25
54...	15.00	5.00			10.00		30
Total...	$302.79	$254.79			$48.00		347

C. ACTIVITIES

I. "There should be at least 120 minutes per week spent in actual rehearsal; more time is necessary for the best results."

TABLE VII

TIME SPENT AT BAND REHEARSAL PER COLLEGE YEAR OF NINE MONTHS

Group	Number of Bands	Number of weeks of regular rehearsals during 9 months	FIRST CONCERT BAND				SECOND BAND				R.O.T.C. OR MILITARY			
			Number of rehearsals per week	Length of time per rehearsal, in minutes	Total minutes per week spent in band rehearsal	Total hours per year spent in band rehearsal	Number of rehearsals per week	Length of time per rehearsal, in minutes	Total minutes per week spent in band rehearsal	Total hours per year spent in band rehearsal	Number of rehearsals per week	Length of time per rehearsal, in minutes	Total minutes per week spent in band rehearsal	Total hours per year spent in band rehearsal
	1	32	3	60	180	96	·							
	1	36	5	50	250	150								
	1	32	2	60	120	64								
	3	36	2	60	120	72	1	150	150	90	2	50	100	60
	2	36	2	90	180	108					1	90	90	54
	1	36	1	90	90	54								
	1	36	1	120	120	72								
	1	32	1	120	120	64								
	1	36	3	60	180	108								
	1	36	1	120	120	72								
	2	36	2	120	240	144					1	120	120	72
Group I	3	36	4	50	200	120	2	50	100	60	2	50	100	60
	1	34	2	75	150	85								
	1	34	2	60	120	68								
	1	36	2	90	180	108								
	3	36	2	75	150	90	1	75	75	45	2	75	150	90
	3	36	4	50	200	120	3	50	150	90	3	50	150	90
	1	36	3	75	225	135								
	2	30	1	120	120	60					1	120	120	60
	2	36	2	75	150	90	2	75	150	90				
	1	36	1	120	120	72								
	2	36	3	60	180	108	2	60	120	72				
	2	36	1	90	90	54					1	90	90	54
	2	36	1	110	110	66					1	110	110	66
	1	36	1	120	120	72								
MEDIAN		36	2	75	150	85	2	67.5	135	81	1	90	110	60
RANGE		30–36	1–5	50–120	90–250	54–150	1–3	50–150	75–150	45–90	1–3	50–120	90–150	54–90

TABLE VII—*Continued*

Group	Number of Bands	Number of weeks of regular rehearsals during 9 months	FIRST CONCERT BAND				SECOND BAND				R.O.T.C. OR MILITARY			
			Number of rehearsals per week	Length of time per rehearsal, in minutes	Total minutes per week spent in band rehearsal	Total hours per year spent in band rehearsal	Number of rehearsals per week	Length of time per rehearsal, in minutes	Total minutes per week spent in band rehearsal	Total hours per year spent in band rehearsal	Number of rehearsals per week	Length of time per rehearsal, in minutes	Total minutes per week spent in band rehearsal	Total hours per year spent in band rehearsal
Group II	3	32	3	60	180	96	3	60	180	96	3	60	180	96
	1	36									4	45	180	108
	1	36									3	60	180	108
	1	34									3	60	180	102
	1	36									3	50	150	90
	3	36	2	90	180	108	2	90	180	108	1	90	90	54
	2	34	3	60	180	102					1	60	60	34
	2	30	1	90	90	45					1	60	60	30
	2	32	3	60	180	96					3	60	180	96
	1	34									3	60	180	102
	1	36									4	50	200	120
	2	34	2	105	210	119					2	105	210	119
	2	35	2	60	120	70					2	60	120	70
	2	36	5	50	250	150					3	45	135	81
	1	36	3	90	270	162								
	1	36									2	90	180	108
	1	33									2	120	240	132
	3	30	2	75	150	75	2	75	150	75	2	75	150	75
	1	33	2	90	180	99								
MEDIAN		34	2	75	180	99	2	75	180	96	3	60	180	96
RANGE		30–36	1–5	50–105	90–270	45–162	2–3	60–90	150–180	75–108	1–4	45–120	60–240	30–132
Group III	2	44	1	90	90	66	1	90	90	66				
	2	36	2	60	120	72	2	60	120	72				
	1	36	4	60	240	144								
	2	36	1	120	120	72	1	120	120	72				
	1	34	2	40	80	45								
	1	36	2	45	90	54								
	1	36	2	50	100	60								
	1	48	2	60	120	96								
	1	36	4	2–55 2–90	290	174								
	1	30	2	90	180	90								
MEDIAN		36	2	60	120	72	1	90	120	72				
RANGE		30–48	1–4	40–120	80–290	45–174	1–2	60–120	90–120	66–72				

The result of the projection of the colleges against this standard is shown in Table VII. The number of colleges which are definitely below standard is indicated in the following tabulation.

	First Concert Band		*Second Band*		*R.O.T.C. or Military*	
Group	Total minutes per wk. spent in band rehearsal	Total hours per yr. spent in band rehearsal	Total minutes per wk. spent in band rehearsal	Total hours per yr. spent in band rehearsal	Total minutes per wk. spent in band rehearsal	Total hours per yr. spent in band rehearsal
I.........	3	7	2	2	5	6
II........	1	2	..	..	3	4
III.......	4	4	1	1	..	..

II. "The functions at which the bands play should be limited." The status of the colleges on this standard is shown in Tables VIII and IX, Table VIII indicating the total number of times that all bands play at various functions and Table IX covering the same point for the 17 colleges and universities that have both a concert and a military band.

Some of the most outstanding facts as shown in Table IX may be summarized as follows:

Football games, while essentially a function of the R.O.T.C. or military band, were handled in 29 per cent of the total appearances by the first concert band.

Basketball games, again essentially a function of the R.O.T.C. or military band, were handled by the first concert band in 25.6 per cent of the total appearances.

Track meets, a function of the R.O.T.C. or military band, were handled in 31.4 per cent of the appearances by the first concert band.

Baseball games, also a function of the R.O.T.C. or military band, were handled in 34.1 per cent of the appearances by the first concert band.

A differentiation in bands for pep meetings is very difficult to make because in many cases a short concert is given beforehand, so that this might easily be considered a function of either the first concert or the military band.

Pep parades before and after games, while essentially a func-

TABLE VIII

FUNCTIONS AT WHICH COLLEGE AND UNIVERSITY BANDS PLAY—TOTAL APPEARANCES

Functions	Combined Bands			First Concert Band			Second Band			R.O.T.C or Military Band		Total
	Group I	Group II	Group III	Group I	Group II	Group III	Group I	Group II	Group III	Group I	Group II	
Football Games	7	24	6	107	15	47	2		4	50	106	368
Basketball Games		19	12	96	39	65	22		8	57	110	428
Wrestling Meets		12		5	3		3				5	28
Track Meets		6		24	9	6	3		2	5	14	69
Baseball Games		9		30	20	14	4	1		18	37	133
Pep Meetings		7	5	55	37	30	16	4	4	45	63	266
Pep Parades—Before and after Games		4		54	18	23	9	2	4	27	60	201
Political Meetings on Campus				7	1					2	8	18
Convocations	4			28	18	12		3		11	10	91
Assemblies	4	8		25	29	23			1	6	23	114
Graduation Exercises	2			12	8	6				3	4	35
Spring Open Air Concerts				70	43	39						152
Special Concerts with Paid Admission	3			143	25	17				9	5	202
Dedication Exercises—All Kinds	2	3		20	6	14				5	39	89
Spring Carnivals, Campfires, Picnics, etc.	2	2		8	7	3				5	5	32
Receptions		5		4	4							13
Dinners				5	3							8
Water Carnival				3								3
Radio Broadcasting					10						6	16
Drill and R. O. T. C. Functions										45	219	264
Miscellaneous Playing				51	22	11		12		10		106
TOTAL APPEARANCES	24	99	23	747	317	310	59	22	23	298	714	2,636

TABLE IX

BANDS USED WHERE COLLEGE OR UNIVERSITY HAD TWO OR MORE BANDS INCLUDING BOTH CONCERT AND MILITARY —

TOTAL APPEARANCES

FUNCTIONS	First Concert Band	R.O.T.C. or Military Band	Second Band	Combined-Bands
Football Games	30	73	2	20
Basketball Games	21	61	14	21
Wrestling Meets	1	7		11
Track Meets	7	15	3	4
Baseball Games	15	29	5	9
Pep Meetings	28	67	13	4
Pep Parades Before or After Games	20	45	6	2
Political Meetings on Campus	1	2		
Convocations	27	13		8
Assemblies	24	10	3	3
Graduation Exercises	10	4	1	1
Spring Open Air Concerts	41	9	3	4
Special Concerts with Paid Admission	145	6		3
Dedication Exercises—All Kinds	9	5		3
Spring Carnivals, Campfires, Picnics, etc.	2	7		2
Receptions				5
Radio Broadcasting	10	8		
Miscellaneous Playing	37	45	1	

tion of the R.O.T.C. or military band, were handled in **30.1** per cent of the total appearances by the first concert band.

Convocations, which should be considered a function of the first concert band, were handled in **32.5** per cent of the appearances by the R.O.T.C. or military band.

Similarly, assemblies, a function of the first concert band, were handled in **29.4** per cent of the appearances by the military band.

Graduation exercises, also a function of the first concert band, were handled by the R.O.T.C. or military band in **28.6** per cent of the total appearances.

Spring open air concerts, a definite function of the concert band, were held in **18** per cent of the total appearances under the auspices of the R.O.T.C. or military band.

Dedication exercises of all kinds may be a function of either the concert or military band, depending on whether the playing is done inside or outside.

Radio broadcasting, which should have been handled in this group of institutions by the concert band, except in rare instances, was handled by the R.O.T.C. or military band in 44.4 per cent of the total broadcasting of the year.

Under "miscellaneous playing," we find appearances of both concert and military bands, and these appearances, on consultation of the original sources, seem to be in keeping with our standard.

III. "Concert trips, where possible, should be arranged for the Concert Band in order to increase interest and furnish an incentive for careful musical work and the development of well-rounded programs." When the colleges were projected against this standard, the following result was noted:

Group I................................. 12, or 40 per cent.
Group II................................ 7, or 36.8 per cent.
Group III............................... No trips taken.

Considering the entire group of 54 bands, we have 19, or 35.2 per cent, making trips during the year.

IV. "Free open air concerts by the Concert Band, or a combination of bands, should be given in the spring as soon as the weather permits." The tabulation for the three groups appears as follows:

Group I................................. 15, or 60 per cent.
Group II................................ 15, or 78.9 per cent.
Group III............................... 8, or 80 per cent.

Consolidating the three groups, we find that 38, or 70.3 per cent of the bands, give free open air concerts in the spring.

V. "Where possible, an Honorary Society or Fraternity should be sponsored to add incentive for service beyond the Military Band." The colleges as projected against this standard are summarized in Table X. This table shows that 1 institution, or 4 per cent, in Group I has a band fraternity; and 4 institutions, or 21 per cent, in Group II have band fraternities.

TABLE X

DEVICES USED TO KEEP BAND MEMBERS ACTIVE IN BAND WORK THE FULL
FOUR YEARS OF COLLEGE

DEVICES USED	Group I	Group II	Group III
Regular Student Activities.....................	1		
None..	3	6	4
Rebate on Tuition.............................	1		
Sweater Awards...............................	1		
Keys or Medals for Band Service...............	1	1	2
University Blanket for Four Years' Work.........		1	
College Credit Last Two Years..................		2	
Out of Town Trips.............................		2	
Pins or Fobs..................................			1
School Spirit, Pride in Organization.............			1
School Spirit, Learning New Instruments, Concerts, Athletic Contests............................			1
Annual Concert Tours, Sweater, Football Trips, Kappa Kappa Psi..................................		1	
Incidental Fees Refunded, Band Medal, Graduation Banquet......................................		1	
Playing Good Music—Concerts over the State......		1	
Hard Work and Lots of It—Phi Mu Alpha..........		1	
Spring Tour of State for Two Weeks—Kappa Kappa Psi...		1	
Trips with Athletic Teams—Kappa Kappa Psi.......		1	
College Spirit Back of It, Band Medals, Athletic Trips		1	
Football, Trips, Concert Tour, Band Sweater or Watch Charm, Annual Band Formal Dance..............	1		
New Music and Public Performance................	2		
Tradition Strong, History Thirty-five Years, Seven Hundred Active Alumni, Best Students in It.......	1		
New Uniforms Every Year, Concerts, Music, Parties, Tours, Snappy Rehearsals......................	1		
Standard Classics for Study—Band Key............	1		
Discipline and Playing a Good Grade of Music......	1		
Athletic Events, Student Body Affairs, Broadcasting, and Concerts.................................	1		
Concerts, Athletic Events......................	1		1
Trips, Athletic Contests and Concerts, Band Fraternity	1		
Interest in Concert Band, Five Tours.............	1		
Tuition Refunded and Credit—Junior and Senior Year	1		
Good Leader, Good Music—Two or Three Trips Every Year..	2		
Fifty Dollars for Year's Work, Athletic Contests, Out of Town Trips...............................	1		
Chapel Concerts, Home Football Games, Football Trips, Basketball Games......................	1		
New Music, Trips, Band Socials, and Medals for Service	1		
Increase of Pay, Seniority in Position at Games, Lockers, etc..................................	1		

TABLE XI

Fund or Funds Used by Colleges and Universities to Purchase Instruments

Funds Used to Purchase Instruments	Group I	Group II	Group III
Special Appropriation of College or State	5	1	
Alumni of University	1		
Military Department		1	
Music Department		1	1
Association of Students' Fund	1		
Equipment Fund	2		
General Fund	2	6	1
Fund from Concerts and Earnings	1	1	
Music Union of the College	1		
Music Revolving Fund	1		
Fee Added to Student Tuition	2	1	
Band Budget	2		
Student Chest or Fund		1	
Student Activity Fee		1	1
United States Government—Army		1	
General Fund, Fund from Concerts			1
Military Department, Music Department, Association of Students, United States Government	1		
Popular Subscription, Fund from Concerts	1		
Special Appropriation, Student Athletic Fund	1		
Fund from Concerts, Band Budget, Band Dances, Alumni of Band	1		
Special Appropriation, Student Chest	1		
Don't Know	1	1	
No Instruments Owned by University	1	1	
Equipment Fund, Music Council Funds		1	
Contingent Fund			3
Equipment Fund, Popular Subscription		1	
United States Government, Arts Fund		1	
Music Department, Local Chamber of Commerce			1
Equipment Fund, General Fund			1
Music Department, Fund from Concerts, Clubs of College			1

D. Financing

I. "All financial matters should be handled through the Bursar's or Treasurer's office." The three groups were found to conform to this standard as follows:

Group I .... 15, or 60 per cent.

Group II .... 7, or 36.8 per cent.

Group III .... 2, or 20 per cent.

Considering all three groups, we find that 24 out of 54, or 44.4 per cent, handle their financial affairs through the bursar's office.

II. "A regular budget should be provided in which provision is made for:

1. "The purchase of new instruments as needed by the band." The colleges projected against this standard are shown in Table XI. Out of the entire 54 bands only 2 in Group I indicated a band budget provision for the purchase of new instruments as needed.

2. "The repair of instruments owned by the college or university." The colleges projected against this standard are shown in Table XII. From this table we find that 3 bands in Group I have a regular budget provision and 2 in Group II have a similar provision.

3. "The purchase of new music as needed for the band. A minimum of $50.00 annually for each multiple of 25 men in band work is a reasonable standard." Tables XIII and XIV show the projection of the colleges against this point. In Table XIII we find that 24 out of 54 of the bands indicated that there was no limit to the amount they could spend for music annually. The remaining 30 bands stated that they were limited as to the amount they could spend, 22 of the 30 giving figures which could be checked against the standard. Of these 22, 19 were definitely below standard. In Table XIV we find that 2 bands in the first group have a band budget provision covering music and 1 band in the second group has such a provision.

4. "The replacement of old instruments at regular periods." Table XV shows the three groups of colleges projected against this standard. Three colleges in Group I have a budget allowance or regular budget provision for the replacement of old instruments. Two bands in Group II and I band in Group III also meet this standard. Out of the 54 bands we find 6 with a budget provision covering this point.

5. "The purchase and replacement of uniforms as needed." The colleges projected against this standard are shown in Table XVI. Out of the 54 bands included in the

TABLE XII

PROVISION MADE FOR REPAIRING AND OVERHAULING INSTRUMENTS OWNED
BY COLLEGE OR UNIVERSITY

FUND	Group I	Group II	Group III
$300 Annually for Repairs, Music, and Incidentals....	1		
Special Appropriation When Necessary..............	7	1	
None..	7	6	2
Income from Concerts.............................	1		
About all Requisitioned by Director................	1	1	
Budget Allowance in Maintenance Fund.............	1		
Regular Budget Provision.........................	3	2	
Music Revolving Fund............................	1		
Instruments Repaired Each Summer by College......		1	
War Dept. Requires Instruments be Kept in Repair..		1	
Paid for by Students..............................		1	
Registrar Budget.................................		1	
General Fund.....................................		2	
Music Department Budget.........................		1	1
Only Very Worst Repairs Handled by College........		1	
Requisition through State.........................			3
Contingent Fund.................................			1
Rent of Instruments Pays Repairs. Students Pay Damage...			1
Annual Appropriation.............................			1
Military Dept. $50, Music Dept. $50, Association of Students $100...................................	1		
$30 a Year.......................................	1		
$25 a Year.......................................	1		
$250 Yearly......................................		1	
$50–$100 a Year..................................			1

TABLE XIII

LIMIT OF AMOUNTS SPENT FOR BAND MUSIC ANNUALLY IN SELECTED
COLLEGES, UNIVERSITIES, AND NORMAL SCHOOLS AND TEACHERS
COLLEGES

Group I	Group II	Group III	Upper Limit of Amounts Spent Annually	Minimum That Should be Allowed	Total Number of Band Men in College Bands	No. of Bands in Each College or University
10	8	6	No Limit			
1			$ 80.00	$100.00	47	1
1			$200.00	$350.00	172	2
1			Student Council Fixes			1
1			$ 70.00	$150.00	56	1
1	/		$ 75.00	$150.00	66	1
1			$100.00	$150.00	65	1
1			$ 40.00	$100.00	49	1
1			$ 30.00	$100.00	32	1
1			Budget Account			
1			$100.00	$300.00	135	3
1			Director Furnishes			
1			Amount Earned			
1			$300.00	$250.00	123	1
1			Director's Account			
1			$100.00	$150.00	66	2
	1		$ 15.00	$100.00	39	1
	1		......			
	1		Band Treasury			
	1		$ 50.00	$100.00	34	1
	1		$250.00	$250.00	125	2
	1		$100.00	$200.00	88	2
	1		$100.00	$300.00	142	3
	1		$100.00	$150.00	78	2
	1		$ 25.00	$150.00	56	1
	1		$125.00	$450.00	221	3
	1		$150.00	$150.00	64	1
		1	$ 25.00	$100.00	54	1
		1	$ 45.00	$ 50.00	27	1
		1	......			
		1	$ 60.00	$150.00	36	1

TABLE XIV
Funds Used for Purchase of Band Music

Funds	Group I	Group II	Group III
University Athletic Association...................	1		
University or College Funds......................	7	8	
General Fund..................................			10
Student Fund..................................	1		
Military Department............................	1		
Income from Concerts and Other Work.............	1	1	
Music Department..............................	3	2	
Music Union...................................	1		
Annual University Appropriation..................	1	1	
Director Furnishes It...........................	2		
Student Fees Added to Tuition....................	1		
Band Budget...................................	2	1	
Student Activity Fund...........................		1	
Music Council..................................		1	
Student Body..................................		1	
University and Army............................		1	
University and Military Department...............		1	
University Funds, University Athletic Association....		1	
Band from Concerts, $2 Fee Assessed Members......	1		
Student Council out of Activity Fee...............	1		
Music Dept., Military Dept., Association of Students	1		
Music Department, Earnings of Band..............	1		

TABLE XV
Funds Used for Purchase of Instruments

Funds	Group I	Group II	Group III
Special Appropriation............................	6	1	1
None..	9	13	1
Can Be Purchased as Needed......................	2		
Furnished by Music Union........................	1		
No Regular Provision, Take up Special Cases........	1		
Music Revolving Fund...........................	1		
Regular Budget.................................	1	2	1
Budget Allowance, Varying from Year to Year as Needed.......................................	2		
Through Purchasing Agent........................		1	
Very Little, What Is Left Over at End of Year from Music Budget Dept.............................		1	
Music Department Supplies.......................		1	
State Funds by Requisition.......................			2
Music Department Budget........................			3
Contingent Fund................................			1
Annual Appropriation............................			1
$400 (not annually)..............................	1		
Music Dept. $1000, Assoc. of Students $600 a Year....	1		

TABLE XVI

FUNDS OUT OF WHICH COLLEGE PURCHASED UNIFORMS OR PARTS OF UNIFORMS

FUND OR FUNDS USED	Group I	Group II	Group III
College Athletic Association........................	2		
Special Appropriation............................	3		
Alumni...	1		
Association of Students..........................	1	1	
Equipment Fund.................................	1		
Student Funds...................................	1	1	
General Fund....................................	1	3	2
Students Buy Their Own..........................	4	4	1
Fee Added to Students' Tuition....................	1		
Band Budget Furnished by University..............	2		
No Regular Fund Provided........................	1		
Band Uniform Fund..............................		1	
Army—United States Government.................		3	
Don't Know.....................................		1	
Contingent Fund.................................			2
State Funds.....................................			2
Music Department Funds.........................			1
Band Concerts and Organization Gifts..............			1
General Activity, Maintenance Fund...............			1
Student Subscription, College Athletic Association....		1	
Capes Given by President.........................		1	
Maintenance and Student Collections..............		1	
Students and Army...............................		2	
General Fund and Student Chest...................	1		
Band Budget, Band Earnings, Alumni of Band.......	1		
Part of Students' Fees Appropriated For Band, Band Earnings....................................	1		
Special Fund, Student Athletic Association..........	1		
Popular Subscription, $100, General Fund...........	1		
Popular Subscription, Fund from Concerts..........	1		
Student Activity Fee, Alumni, Athletic Association..	1		

study only 2 in Group I have a band budget provision
for the purchase of uniforms.

6. and 7. "The depreciation to charge off on band instruments and uniforms owned by the college." No figures
are available covering depreciation to charge off on
band instruments and uniforms; hence this point could
not be covered in the survey of the colleges.

8. "The bond of the Business Manager of the band."
This question was not included in the original survey
and hence we have no information covering it.

E. College Credit

IV. "College credit should be allowed for band work on the basis
of:

1. Time put in at rehearsals or other regular scheduled
work of the band which may be called educational."
The colleges were projected against this standard with
the following result:

Group I................................... 9, or 36 per cent.
Group II................................... 7, or 36.8 per cent.
Group III................................... 3, or 30 per cent.

Out of the 54 bands, 19, or 35.2 per cent meet this
standard.

2. "Improvement of the men during the year on their respective instruments." Measured against this standard
the colleges appear as follows:

Group I................................... 4, or 16 per cent.
Group II................................... 4, or 21 per cent.
Group III................................... 4, or 40 per cent.

This indicates that 12 out of 54 bands, or 22.2 per cent,
meet this standard.

CHAPTER IV

GENERAL SUMMARY

A. Personnel

We find from a consideration of "Personnel" under Chapter III that the functions of the director are in most cases adequately cared for as provided by our standards. In 77.7 per cent of the total institutions the director is a member of the music department.

There seems to be some confusion between the duties of the director and the duties of the business manager. The director should coöperate with the business manager in making business arrangements for all appearances of the band rather than assume these duties. A clearer differentiation of function on this point should be made.

Lessons given through the music department, where a department exists, should include class instruction to supplement private instruction and should interest a larger group in instrumental work.

The study reveals that the function of the student officers in relation to the band is much less clearly defined, especially in the normal schools and teachers colleges where student officers, such as business managers, are either lacking entirely or limited in the functions that they perform. Although there is fairly close agreement as to the major duties to be performed by the student officers, there is some divergence of opinion as to which student officer should perform the various duties. These functions should be clearly set forth in the constitution and by-laws and should apply to officers in all three groups of institutions. In general, except where a large number of the functions of student officers are grouped under one individual, the student officers of the band should not be paid for their services. Rebating tuition and giving scholarships to band members are highly questionable practices and should be unnecessary where college credit is allowed and the devices are used, as indicated later in the summary, to keep band members active.

B. Equipment

Under "Equipment" we find that in Table V A there is considerable discrepancy as to the colleges that furnish at least a part of the instruments listed in this table. If the full possibilities of the symphonic band are realized, these instruments must be provided for students. Where it is impossible to furnish instruments free of charge, they should be made available through rental. The main thing is to have the instruments available. A deposit should be required on all instruments and uniforms furnished free to students to insure prompt return and facilitate adjustment in case of damage. The deposit on instruments and equipment, together with the bond furnished by the business manager, will insure care and accuracy in the handling of band equipment.

From Table VI we see that none of the institutions rent uniforms to students. Parts of the uniform which may be used only at college functions, like football equipment, etc., should be furnished free. Of the total cost of all uniforms used at the 54 institutions, approximately 20 per cent is borne by the student and the other 80 per cent is furnished free through some college facility. The part of the cost borne by the student applies largely to those articles of uniform the use of which is not limited to band functions.

C. Activities

Table VII reveals the fact that the three groups of bands are up to standard in the amount of time spent at band rehearsal per week, while Groups I and II are well above the standard. It would seem that 180 minutes per week in the case of Groups I and II should be set as a standard rather than 120 minutes.

From Tables VIII and IX it would appear that there should be a clearer differentiation of function between the concert and military bands. Even where there are two bands, as shown in Table IX, this difference is not clearly understood. Each type of band has a distinct function to perform in college and the band should be used which will best serve the engagement.

Many institutions do not provide concert trips for their concert band. Group III is particularly weak in this regard, as no concert trips were provided by the ten institutions. This type of activity needs to be strengthened in the three groups of institutions. A high standard of musical attainment should be secured and this outlet provided, which will stimulate interest of alumni, future students, patrons of the college, and band members.

Free open air concerts are provided by a majority of the institutions. The rest should undoubtedly make provision for these concerts as they, too, are a fine means of publicity and an incentive to band members. Concert trips and free open air concerts in the spring give an objective for the development of a high musical standard. In addition they help to hold the band together throughout the year.

From Table X we find that one institution in Group I and four institutions in Group II have an honorary fraternity. Where an honorary fraternity or society is sponsored, a large number of the devices used to keep band members active are taken care of through the organization or are found to be unnecessary. In many institutions some form of honorary fraternity or society could be sponsored with profit. A strong band alumni association, similar to that of Stanford University, would aid greatly in increasing the interest in and the prestige of the band. Rebate on tuition is a questionable practice to foster for any student organization. A large number of the devices used to keep band members active, as indicated in Table X, such as pins, fobs, blankets, sweaters, etc., will be found unnecessary if the band has a balanced year-round program, and the above inducements are sponsored.

D. Financing

Under the standard which provides for financial matters being handled through the bursar's or treasurer's office, we find that only 44.4 per cent of the entire number of bands have their finances cared for in this way. The bursar's or treasurer's office is equipped to take care of the financial business of the college and with a definite band budget there should be no objection to its being handled in this manner. We find the regular budget plan for college bands still in the experimental stage. Perhaps this has been due to the fact that we have had no figures available for estimating the length of life of uniforms and instruments, and their annual repair and depreciation charge. We find only two institutions making budget provision for the purchase of new instruments. These various funds, as indicated in Table XI, should be centralized in the budget. Five bands out of 54 have a budget provision for the repair of instruments owned by the college or university, as shown in Table XII. Band instrument companies report that institutions usually send in instruments and ask that they be repaired as cheaply as possible, since no provision has been made for repair and it must be handled by special appropriation. There is no longer any excuse for such lack of business methods, since the amount needed for the annual repair of a set of instruments may be easily determined from Table XVII. Only three of the entire 54 bands indicated a budget provision for music and 19 institutions are definitely below standard, as shown by Table XIII. Six of the 54 bands have a budget provision for the replacement of old instruments at regular periods. Accurate figures are now available for the determining of budget needs on instruments, as shown in Table XVII, Appendix A. The total years of service to be expected from all types of instruments are set forth, the annual amount to place in the budget for repairs has been determined, and the depreciation to charge off on instruments is included. Two out of 54 of the colleges have a budget provision for the purchase and replacement of uniforms as needed. This indicates a marked need for careful budgeting. The total years of service, the annual charge to make for cleaning and repair, and the amount to charge off as depreciation have been tabulated in Table XVIII, Appendix B. Tables XVII and XVIII will make it possible for any band to be placed on an accurate budget basis. Instead of scattered and haphazard support the various funds should be united into an adequate annual budget that will consider present and future needs of the band.

E. College Credit

From Table III it is seen that 35.2 per cent of the institutions allow band credit as a free elective on all courses of the college or university. College credit is allowed for band work as a free elective on music and arts courses by 22.2 per cent of the institutions. In giving college credit for band work, at least three factors should be considered:

(1) The amount of time spent at rehearsal should be used as

a basis for estimating the total hours of credit. Two hours per week for 18 weeks would equal one semester hour's credit.

(2) Written tests and playing tests should be given as a basis for grading and determining improvement. Private and group lessons carried by the students throughout the year may take the place of these tests. The student that does not show definite improvement as the year advances should receive a low grade or be dropped entirely.

(3) The presence of the men at all functions at which the band plays should receive some consideration in the grade given. To justify credit being allowed for band work, a high academic standard must be maintained in keeping with other academic subjects of the institution. From the need for credit as shown in Chapter II and the present practice of allowing music credit in high schools and colleges, it appears that there should be an extension of college credit allowed for band work as a free elective on all courses of the college or university.

CHAPTER V

RECOMMENDATIONS

The following recommendations appear necessary in the light of the findings revealed in Chapters II and III and the General Summary.

A. Personnel

The director of the band should be a member of the music department, where one exists, in order to have all musical organizations coördinated in a comprehensive program of applied music on the campus. Where no music department exists there should be a central organization to unite the effort of the band and other musical organizations on the campus, such as a Music Union or Music Council. The director of the band should be in charge of all band activity, and while it will be found necessary and desirable to transfer many duties to student officers the director must be held responsible for the activity and proper functioning of the band. He should have direct charge of the band at all functions at which the band plays, except in emergency. He should make requisition on the band budget through the bursar's office for the purchase of new music, instruments, uniforms, and supplies as needed for the band. He should make requisition in a similar manner for the repair of instruments and equipment, replacement of instruments and equipment as provided for in the budget, and the replacement and repair of uniforms as needed. The director should coöperate with the business manager in making business arrangements for all appearances of the band rather than assume these duties. The director should give, or arrange to have given, through the music department if there is one, both private and class instruction on band instruments.

The duties of student officers should be clearly stated in the constitution and by-laws or R.O.T.C. regulations in order to avoid confusion and overlapping of duties. The five usual stu-

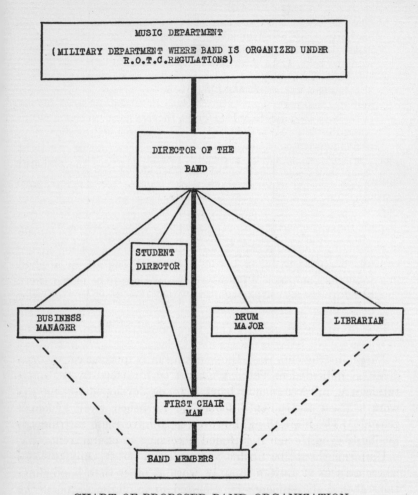

CHART OF PROPOSED BAND ORGANIZATION

dent officers are Student Director, Business Manager, Librarian,
First Chair Man on Each Section, and Drum Major. The approximate functions to be performed by each may be summarized
as follows:

a) The student director should be in charge of the band in the absence
of the director. He should arrange for sections rehearsals under the
guidance of the director and take roll of the band at rehearsals and
at all functions where the band plays. He should assist the director
at all times and be his "right-hand man."

b) The business manager should arrange for the transportation of men and instruments at all functions at which the band plays, as well as make the business arrangements for all appearances of the band, with the help of the director. He should consult with the director and bursar in making arrangements for the spring tour of the band. The business manager should have complete charge of instruments, uniforms, and other equipment, checking them out and in as needed. Other band members may help him in the last named function but he is responsible for a careful check of the condition and location of all band equipment.

c) The librarian should have complete charge of all band music and should index and file it under the guidance of the director. The librarian should make up march books with the help of other band men and place music on the stands at rehearsal or concert.

d) The first chair man should help others in his section who are having difficulty with their parts. This should be done at section rehearsal where he will be in charge. When the first chair man is experienced he may greatly aid the director in helping to place men on parts.

e) The drum major should have complete charge of the band at all times when on parade. The designation of music to be played should be left to the student director, where the drum major is not a musician, otherwise he must remain in full charge.

B. EQUIPMENT

Large instruments and those not usually purchased by students, as indicated in Table VA, must be furnished by the institution if a full symphonic band is to be developed for concert work. These instruments should be furnished free, whenever possible. The main thing, however, is to have these instruments available even though it is found necessary to charge rental.

Uniforms should be furnished free to students. Only in cases where articles of uniform may be worn at other than band functions should the students be required to purchase parts of the uniform, or the entire uniform in case of tuxedos.

A deposit of not less than $10.00 on instruments and $5.00 on uniforms should be required where equipment is furnished free to students. This deposit, together with the bond under which the business manager is placed, will insure careful and accurate handling of all band equipment.

C. ACTIVITIES

Since the best college and university bands, as indicated by Table VII and the original data, spend from **180** to **290** minutes per week in actual rehearsal time, the standard set up of 120 minutes per week should be held as an absolute minimum below which no band should be allowed to go.

It is difficult, with the musicians found in college bands, to develop one band which can handle both concert and military functions. For that reason it is necessary to determine which type of band is to be developed and then limit the functions at which the band plays to those which it can handle best. These functions have been set up in Chapter II and need not be repeated here. The ideal situation is to have both a concert or symphonic band and a military band with at least one band organized as a "feeder" for the two major organizations. There are enough functions which demand both types of band work at colleges and universities, as shown by Tables VIII and IX, to justify both types of band, and in most of the institutions there are band men enough for two types of organizations.

Concert trips and free open air concerts should be sponsored by every concert band. High standards of performance must be developed that will advertise the institution, attract new students, gain the hearty support of alumni and patrons, build college spirit, and develop musical appreciation on the part of the student body. Such a band is invaluable to any institution.

Where possible, an honorary society or fraternity, to which band members are eligible, should be sponsored to add incentive for service beyond the first two years of military band work. Such an organization placed as a goal for active, faithful service toward the end of the four years' work in band represents one of the strongest incentives to hold and keep the band men active throughout their college life.

D. FINANCING

All financial matters pertaining to the band should be handled through the bursar's or treasurer's office, where requisition may be drawn on the band budget as needed. Instead of the present hit-and-miss systems of financing, as indicated in Tables XI to XVI, an adequate annual budget should be provided that takes care of the following items:

  a) The purchase of new instruments as needed by the band. This will be determined by the future program as well as by the yearly program which is determined on.

b) The repair of instruments owned by the college. A list should be made of the instruments owned by the institution and from this the annual amount needed to keep each instrument in good repair may be easily determined by consulting Table XVII, column 2.

c) The purchase of new music as needed by the band should be included. A minimum of $50.00 for each multiple of 25 men in band work should be placed in the budget.

d) The replacement of old instruments as needed. The number of years of service which may be expected from instruments under college band conditions may be determined by consulting column 1 of Table XVII. When an instrument has given the number of years of service, as indicated in this table, provision should be made for replacing it with a new one.

e) The amount needed for the purchase of new uniforms should appear in the budget. Replacement of uniforms may be figured from Table XVII by consulting column 2. When the year's service, which is indicated in column 2, has been received, there must be a budget provision for replacement.

f) The depreciation to charge off on band instruments may be determined from Table XVII. The age of the instrument should be determined, then the per cent of the original value which is to be carried on the books may be determined by multiplying the per cent of depreciation as indicated in columns 3-8 by the original cost of the instrument.

g) The depreciation to charge off on uniforms may be determined from Table XVIII, columns 3-7. The per cent of the original value to be carried on the books may be determined in a manner similar to (*f*).

h) The bond of the business manager should be carried as a band expense in the budget.

Through the use of Tables XVII and XVIII any band may be placed on an accurate budget basis. Before making out a budget, a band program for the year should be determined and Appendices A and B should be carefully studied.

E. COLLEGE CREDIT

College credit should be allowed for band work, over and above that given for military drill, as a free elective on all courses of the college or university. In giving college credit the factors which should be considered are clearly indicated in Chapter II and the General Summary.

One objection that has been raised to the giving of college credit for band work is the lack of academic preparation of those in charge of band work. That may have been true in the past, but good band men who have not only the baccalaureate degree but graduate degrees as well are now available and will be available in increasing numbers in the future.

A good band is a definitely purchasable commodity. A good director must be secured, who is a good teacher and knows how to handle college students. With a good director, adequate time and place to rehearse, and an adequate yearly budget provision, the writer knows of no place where a fine band cannot be established. With the ever increasing number entering college who have had fine grade and high school band experience, the problem of securing musicians is largely cared for. It will be more and more a problem of how best to use these musicians coming from the public schools, and our college and university bands must act and maintain high standards if they are to offer advanced training in band work.

APPENDIX A

REPLACEMENT AND DEPRECIATION CHARGES FOR BAND INSTRUMENTS

In order to secure accurate data for tables showing replacement and depreciation charges for band instruments, the writer made a personal visit to the following factories. They are listed in the order in which they were visited.

The H. N. White Company, Cleveland, Ohio.
C. G. Conn, Ltd., Elkhart, Indiana.
The Martin Band Instrument Company, Elkhart, Indiana.
Frank Holton Company, Elkhorn, Wisconsin.

Additional data were secured through correspondence with the York Band Instrument Company, Grand Rapids, Michigan; and complete figures were furnished by W. S. Wood, Colonel, Q. M. Corps, War Department, Philadelphia Quartermaster Intermediate Depot, Philadelphia, Pennsylvania.

Very detailed figures were given by each band instrument company covering their experience and business relationships with many university bands. In cases where the company did not manufacture the instrument or was not an agent for some other make of instrument, the figures were omitted. All of the band instrument companies were very much interested in the study and the figures given in many cases represent several days' work on the part of the individuals compiling them.

The figures furnished by the Army were extremely accurate and cover actual accounts of thirty-two bands at the various Army stations.

The figures shown in Table XVII represent the arithmetic mean of the band instrument company figures and those furnished by the Army. The depreciation to be charged off against each instrument and case up to five years and for each year after the five-year period is indicated in the third to eighth columns of Table XVII. Table XVIIA shows the number of times that the average figures of the five band instrument companies were the "same as the Army figures," "above the Army figures," or "below the Army figures." It may be seen from Table XVIIA that on "wood-wind" instruments the average of the band instrument company figures is above that of the Army, while on saxophones, valve instruments, and slide trombones the average figures furnished by the band instrument companies are considerably below those furnished by the Army. This would indicate that the figures furnished by the band instrument companies are more conservative than those furnished by the Army.

The blank used to gather these data was constructed in the same form as Table XVII; hence it is not included in Appendix C.

TABLE XVII
REPLACEMENT AND DEPRECIATION CHARGES FOR BAND INSTRUMENTS

INSTRUMENT	Probable Life of Instrument in yrs.	Annual Charge to Keep Instrument in good repair	Per Cent of Depreciation					
			End of 1st yr. 12 mo.	End of 2nd yr. 24 mo.	End of 3d yr. 36 mo.	End of 4th yr. 48 mo.	End of 5th yr. 60 mo.	Each Year after 5 yrs.
Piccolo (in case) Meyers	6	$ 3.55	35	50	65	80	90	10
Wood Boehm	6	5.15	35	50	65	80	90	10
Silver Boehm	9	5.15	25	36	45	55	64	9
Flute (in case) Meyers	9	4.00	25	36	45	55	64	9
Wood Boehm	9	6.90	25	35	45	55	64	9
Silver Boehm	10	7.65	25	33	40	48	55	9
Oboe (in case) Military	10	7.45	23	32	41	50	60	8
Conservatory	10	8.25	23	32	41	50	60	8
English Horn (in case)								
Military system	11	6.15	22	31	40	49	58	7
Conservatory	11	6.15	22	31	40	49	58	7
Sarrusophone —Brass	13	9.00	17	25	33	42	52	6
Silver-plated	13	9.00	17	25	33	42	52	6
Cases for above	6							
Bassoon								
Conservatory	10	7.65	22	31	40	50	60	8
Case for above	7		40	60	70	80	90	5
E♭ Clarinet—15-4-4	9	5.50	24	35	45	55	64	9
Boehm -17-6	9	6.90	24	35	45	55	64	9
B♭ Clarinet—Albert 15-4-4	9	5.50	24	35	45	55	64	9
Boehm 17-6	9	6.90	24	35	45	55	64	9
Alto Clarinet E♭ Boehm 17-6	9	8.30	24	35	45	55	64	9
Bass Clarinet B♭ Boehm	9	11.60	24	35	45	55	64	9
(17 keys) Case for above	5		50	70	80	90	100	
B♭ Soprano Saxophone Brass	10	8.65	24	36	46	56	65	7
Silver and gold bell	10	8.65	24	36	46	56	65	7
Case for above	6		43	60	73	83	93	7
C Soprano Saxophone Brass	10	8.65	24	36	46	56	65	7
Silver and gold bell	10	8.65	24	36	46	56	65	7
Case for above	6		43	60	73	83	93	7
Alto Saxophone Brass	10	10.25	24	36	46	56	65	7
Silver and gold bell	10	10.25	24	36	46	56	65	7
Cases for above	6		43	60	73	83	93	7
C Melody Saxophone Brass	10	11.25	24	36	46	56	65	7
Silver and gold bell	10	11.25	24	36	46	56	65	7
Case for above	6		43	60	73	83	93	7

TABLE XVII—*Continued*

INSTRUMENT	Prob-able Life of Instrument in yrs.	Annual Charge to Keep Instrument in good repair	Per Cent of Depreciation					
			End of 1st yr. 12 mo.	End of 2nd yr. 24 mo.	End of 3d yr. 36 mo.	End of 4th yr. 48 mo.	End of 5th yr. 60 mo.	Each Year after 5 yrs.
Tenor Saxophone Brass.........	10	$12.65	24	36	46	56	65	7
Silver and gold bell......	10	12.65	24	36	46	56	65	7
Case for above..........	6		43	60	73	83	93	7
E♭ Baritone Saxophone Brass....	10	16.80	24	36	46	56	65	7
Silver and gold bell......	10	16.80	24	36	46	56	65	7
Case for above..........	6		43	60	73	83	93	7
B♭ Bass Saxophone Brass.......	10	22.50	24	36	46	56	65	7
Silver and gold bell......	10	22.50	24	36	46	56	65	7
Case for above..........	6		43	60	73	83	93	7
French Horn—Brass	10	5.60	30	40	49	58	65	7
Silver-plated............	10	5.60	30	40	49	58	65	7
Case for above..........	5		55	70	80	90	100	
E♭ Alto or Mellophone Brass...	10	4.25	30	40	49	58	65	7
Silver-plated............	10	4.25	30	40	49	58	65	7
Case for above..........	5		55	70	80	90	100	
E♭ Cornet Brass...............	9	3.50	34	44	54	63	72	7
Silver and gold bell......	9	3.50	34	44	54	63	72	7
B♭ Cornet and Trumpet Brass.................	10	3.50	30	40	49	58	65	7
Silver and gold bell......	10	3.50	30	40	49	58	65	7
B♭ Tenor Valve Trombone Brass.................	10	4.00	30	40	49	58	65	7
Silver and gold bell......	10	4.00	30	40	49	58	65	7
Case for above..........	5		55	70	80	90	100	
B♭ Tenor Slide Trombone Brass..	8	4.75	32	43	53	63	73	9
Silver and gold bell......	8	4.75	32	43	53	63	73	9
Case for above..........	5		55	70	80	90	100	
Euphonium three valve Brass.................	9	5.85	30	40	50	59	68	8
Silver and gold bell......	9	6.25	30	40	50	59	68	8
Side open case..........	5		55	70	80	90	100	
E♭ Tuba, Medium three valve Brass.................	9	8.65	26	36	46	55	64	9
Silver and gold bell......	9	8.65	26	36	46	55	64	9
Case for above..........	5		55	70	80	90	100	
E♭ Tuba, Monster, upright three valve Brass.............	10	12.60	26	36	44	52	60	8
Silver-plated and gold bell.	10	12.60	26	36	44	52	60	8
Case for above..........	5		55	70	80	90	100	

TABLE XVII—*Continued*

INSTRUMENT	Probable Life of Instrument in yrs.	Annual Charge to Keep Instrument in good repair	Per Cent of Depreciation					
			End of 1st yr. 12 mo.	End of 2nd yr. 24 mo.	End of 3d yr. 36 mo.	End of 4th yr. 48 mo.	End of 5th yr. 60 mo.	Each Year after 5 yrs.
E♭ Tuba, Helicon, Monster three valve Brass........	9	$13.25	27	37	47	56	64	9
Silver-plated............	9	13.25	27	37	47	56	64	9
Trunk for above.........	9		40	50	60	70	80	5
E♭ Sousaphone, bell front, three valve Brass.............	8	14.35	30	40	50	60	70	10
Silver and gold bell......	8	14.35	30	40	50	60	70	10
Trunk for above........	7		35	50	60	70	80	10
BB♭ Bass, Medium, upright, three valve Brass........	9	11.75	30	40	50	60	68	8
Silver and gold bell......	9	11.75	30	40	50	60	68	8
Case for above..........	5		55	70	80	90	100	
BB♭ Bass, Monster, upright, three valve Brass........	9	15.10	30	40	50	60	68	8
Silver and gold bell......	9	15.10	30	40	50	60	68	8
Case for above..........	5		55	70	80	90	100	
BB♭ Bass, Helicon, Monster, three valve Brass........	8	17.40	30	40	50	60	70	10
Silver and gold bell......	8	17.40	30	40	50	60	70	10
Trunk for above........	8		30	40	50	60	70	10
BB♭ Sousaphone, bell front, three valve Brass.............	9	18.10	26	38	50	60	68	8
Silver and gold bell......	9	18.10	26	38	50	60	68	8
Trunk for above........	8		30	40	50	60	70	10
Snare Drums 15″×6″ wood.....	6	4.00	44	58	70	80	90	10
15″×6″ metal S.T.H....	7	4.00	40	50	60	70	80	10
Bass Drums 30″×14″..........	6	9.25	44	58	70	80	90	10
30″×14″ S.T. Head.....	6	9.25	44	58	70	80	90	10
Tympani-Hand screw, two drums, 28″ and 24″............	10	4.80	30	40	50	60	70	6
Pedal T. Two drums.....	10	4.80	30	40	50	60	70	6
Bells and case, round top........	10	1.60	30	40	50	60	70	6
Parsifal bells............	10	1.60	30	40	50	60	70	6
Chimes—set..................	10		30	40	50	60	70	6
Marimbaphones—set...........	8		30	40	50	60	70	10

TABLE XVII A

PROBABLE LIFE OF BAND INSTRUMENTS IN YEARS

(Average figures of five Band Instrument Companies as compared with the United States Army figures)

INSTRUMENTS	Same as Army Figures	Number of Times Average of Band Instrument Companies' Figures Were Above Army Figures				Number of Times Average of Band Instrument Companies' Figures Were Below Army Figures		
		1 yr.	2 yr.	3 yr.	4 yr.	1 yr.	2 yr.	3 yr.
"Wood-wind" Instruments...........	1	11		5	2			
Saxophones.........................							10	4
Valve Instruments and Slide Trombone	3		2			18	7	
Percussion Instruments..............	2	1	2				2	
TOTAL.........................	6	12	2	5	2	18	19	4

APPENDIX B

REPLACEMENT AND DEPRECIATION CHARGES FOR BAND UNIFORMS

In order to secure information for replacement and depreciation charges on band uniforms, a survey blank was made out. This blank appears in Appendix C. Accurate figures were received from the following uniform companies:

1. Stone Uniform Company, 10-12 East 23d Street, New York City.
2. De Moulin Brothers and Company, Greenville, Illinois.
3. National Uniform Company, 12 John Street, New York City.
4. Alexander D'Angelo, 181 Grand Street, New York City.
5. Lilley and Company, Columbus, Ohio.

Where the company did not manufacture the article of uniform as called for, a space was left blank. The figures placed in Table XVIII represent the arithmetic mean of these five companies. The articles of uniform listed in Table XVIII were those used by the 54 university bands included in the study.

TABLE XVIII

REPLACEMENT AND DEPRECIATION CHARGES FOR BAND UNIFORMS

(Based on an average use of twenty-five times per year)

ARTICLE OF UNIFORM	Annual Amount for Cleaning and Repairing	Years of Service to Expect from Article	Percentage of Original Cost to Charge Off as Depreciation				
			End of First Year	End of Second Year	End of Third Year	End of Fourth Year	Each Year After Fourth Year
Helmet...............	$ .65	6	30	53	73	90	5
Band Cap............	.40	5	34	57	77	90	10
Cape................	2.20	6	28	50	69	88	6
Coat................	2.85	5	35	59	80	90	10
O. D. Army Shirt.....	1.00	2	63	100			
Trousers............	2.65	4	44	68	85	100	
Sweater.............	1.20	2	61	100			
Spats...............	.90	3	67	85	100		
Puttees.............	.95	5	41	67	90	95	5
Boots...............	1.50	2	81	100			
Shoes...............	1.65	1	100				
Tuxedo or Full Dress..	3.70	6	29	51	68	82	9
Sam Brown Belt......	.35	6	30	53	72	84	8
Skirt (for Women).....	2.50	6	33	57	75	90	5

APPENDIX C—1

TENTATIVE STANDARDS FOR COLLEGE AND UNIVERSITY BANDS

The Standards listed below have been made up from returns on the Survey blank which you will find inclosed.

If the Standard as stated *is satisfactory*, place a check mark ($\sqrt{}$) in the space provided at the right of the statement.

If the Standard as stated *is not satisfactory*, state briefly what you consider would be a reasonable standard for this point in the space following the statement.

TENTATIVE STANDARDS	SPACE FOR CHECKING STANDARDS
A. PERSONNEL I. The Director of the Band should be a member of the Music Department of the Institution.	
II. The duties of the officers of the band should be clearly stated in the Constitution and By-Laws of the band.	
III. The duties of the officers of the band should be as follows:	
1. DIRECTOR *a)* The Director should have direct charge of the band at all functions at which the band plays.	
b) The Director should make requisitions through the Bursar for: (1) The purchase of new music.	
(2) The purchase of new instruments and supplies for the band.	
(3) The repair of instruments and equipment as needed.	
(4) The replacement of instruments and equipment which are worn out.	
(5) The purchase, replacement and repair of uniforms as needed.	

85

APPENDIX C—1—*Continued*

Tentative Standards—*Continued*	Space for Checking Standards
1. DIRECTOR—*Continued* *c)* The Director should coöperate with the Business Manager in making business arrangements for all appearances of the band. The Director should be responsible for these in the final analysis.	
d) The Director should give instruction on band instruments through the Music Department.	
2. STUDENT DIRECTOR *a)* The Student Director should be in direct charge of the band in the absence of the Director.	
b) The Student Director should arrange for section rehearsals.	
c) The Student Director should take the roll of the band at rehearsals and at all functions where the band plays.	
d) The Student Director should assist the Director at all times.	
3. BUSINESS MANAGER *a)* The Business Manager should arrange for the transportation of men and instruments at all functions at which the band plays.	
b) The Business Manager should have charge of the instruments and uniforms, checking them in and out to the band members as needed.	
c) The Business Manager should make arrangements for the spring tour with the help of the Director and Bursar.	
d) The Business Manager should be responsible for all band equipment, under the Director.	

APPENDIX C—1—*Continued*

TENTATIVE STANDARDS—*Continued*	SPACE FOR CHECKING STANDARDS
3. BUSINESS MANAGER—*Continued* *e*) The Business Manager should give Bond, for the protection of the band, for the return of instruments, uniforms, and equipment. This bond should not be less than $1000 and should be handled through the band budget.	
4. LIBRARIAN *a*) The Librarian should index and file all music, under the direction of the Director.	
b) The Librarian should make up march books and concert folios as needed, with the help of other bandmen.	
c) The Librarian should have complete charge of all band music.	
5. FIRST CHAIR MAN ON EACH SECTION *a*) The First Chair Man should help others in his section who need help.	
b) The First Chair Man should hold section rehearsals for his section as needed.	
c) The First Chair Man should help the Director place the men on parts in his section.	
6. DRUM MAJOR *a*) The Drum Major should have complete charge of the band at all times when on parade.	
IV. No Student officer of the band should be paid for his services.	
B. EQUIPMENT I. The larger instruments and those not usually purchased by students should be furnished by the Institution free of charge.	

APPENDIX C—1—*Continued*

Tentative Standards—*Continued*	Space for Checking Standards
B. Equipment—*Continued* II. Larger instruments and those not usually purchased by students should be rented to students at a nominal fee, at least large enough to cover annual repairs on the set rented.	
III. Students should be required to place a deposit of not less than $10 on instruments furnished free by the college and issued to them.	
IV. Uniforms should be furnished free to members of the band.	
V. Uniforms should be rented to students at a nominal fee, at least large enough to cover cleaning and repair of the uniform for the year.	
VI. A deposit of not less than $5 should be made by each student on the uniform issued to him, where the uniforms are furnished free by the college.	
VII. A deposit of not less than 50c should be made by each student for each march book issued to him.	
C. Activities I. There should be at least 120 minutes per week spent in actual rehearsal; more time is necessary for the best results.	
II. The functions at which the bands play should be limited to: 1. *a*) The Concert Band should handle those functions at which a band may secure the best musical results. Athletic contests, except the big games of the year, marching, parades, reviews, etc., should be left for the Military Band.	
2. *b*) The Military Band should be used for military reviews, marching, most of the athletic contests, and outside work, with the exception of spring open air concerts.	

APPENDIX C—1—*Continued*

TENTATIVE STANDARDS—*Continued*	SPACE FOR CHECKING STANDARDS
C. ACTIVITIES—*Continued* III. Concert trips, where possible, should be arranged for the Concert Band in order to increase interest and furnish an incentive for careful musical work and the development of well rounded programs.	
IV. Free open air concerts by the Concert Band, or a combination of bands, should be given in the spring as soon as the weather permits.	
V. Where possible, an Honorary Society or Fraternity should be sponsored to add incentive for service beyond the military band.	
D. FINANCING I. All financial matters should be handled through the Bursar's or Treasurer's office.	
II. A regular budget should be provided in which provision is made for: 1. The purchase of new instruments as needed by the band.	
2. The repair of instruments owned by the college or university.	
3. The purchase of new music as needed for the band. A minimum of $50 annually for each multiple of 25 men in band work is a reasonable standard.	
4. The replacement of old instruments at regular periods.	
5. The purchase and replacement of uniforms as needed.	
6. The depreciation to charge off on band instruments owned by the college.	
7. The depreciation to charge off on uniforms owned by the college.	
8. The bond of the Business Manager of the band.	

APPENDIX C—1—*Continued*

TENTATIVE STANDARDS—*Continued*	SPACE FOR CHECKING STANDARDS
E. COLLEGE CREDIT NOTE—The following questions have to do with the matter of credit being allowed for band work over and above that given for military drill. I. College credit *should not* be allowed for band work over and above that given for military drill.	
II. College credit *should be allowed* for band work over and above that given for military drill.	
III. College credit should be allowed for band work: 1. As a free elective on all courses of the college or university.	
2. As a free elective on Music and Arts courses offered by the college or university.	
IV. College credit should be allowed for band work on the basis of: 1. Time put in at rehearsals or other regular scheduled work of the band which may be called educational.	
2. Improvement of the men during the year on their respective instruments.	
3. The original ability of the men and their usefulness to the band.	
4. A combination of the above (1, 2, 3). State what combination is best.	
5. Other possibilities as a basis for giving credit. State any that seem good to you.	

Four main groups of functions which bands carry on are recognized as follows:

   a) Those functions in which the main object is publicity for the college or university.
   b) Those functions in which the main object is extra-curricular participation by the students.
   c) Those functions in which the main object is educational for the students concerned.
   d) Those functions in which the main object is financial remuneration for the students concerned or for the band fund of the college or university.

Please place a check mark after each function of the band listed below on the basis of whether you consider it mainly publicity, mainly extra-curricular, mainly educational, or mainly remunerative.

Functions of the College Band	Mainly Publicity	Mainly Extra-Curricular	Mainly Educational	Mainly Remunerative
1. Football Games				
2. Basketball Games				
3. Wrestling Meets				
4. Track Meets				
5. Baseball Games				
6. Pep Meetings				
7. Pep Parades Before and After Games				
8. Political Meetings on the Campus				
9. Convocations and Assemblies				
10. Graduation Exercises				
11. Spring Open Air Concerts				
12. Special Concerts with Paid Admission				
13. Dedication Exercises, All Kinds				
14. Carnivals, Campfires, Picnics, etc. Conducted by the College				
15. Receptions				
16. Dinners, On and Off the Campus				
17. Spring Tours of the Band				
18. Radio Broadcasting by the Band				
19. Playing at County or State Fairs				
20. Regular Rehearsals of the Band				
21. Special Rehearsals in Preparation for Spring Tours, Concerts, etc.				

NOTE—The above list includes all of the activities at which the 54 bands, included in the study, played last year.

SIGNED

Name ....

Address ....

APPENDIX C–2

SURVEY TO DETERMINE THE ORGANIZATION AND ADMINISTRATION OF COLLEGE AND UNIVERSITY BANDS

Two Survey blanks are inclosed. You may keep one for your files.

General

Name of College or University..........................State..........
Is the Director a member of the staff of the Music Department?..........
Please indicate the exact college or university title......................
What is your rank in the Department: Professor, Associate Professor, Assistant Professor, Instructor, Assistant Instructor?......................

Organization and Equipment

Please indicate what part of a band uniform is furnished by each of the three sources, college or university, Army, and students.

Articles in Uniform	Furnished by the College or University		Furnished by the Army for R.O.T.C.	Bought and Used by the Band Members Themselves
	Free of Charge to Students	Rented to Students		
Helmet......................				
Cap—All Types..............				
Cape......................				
Coat......................				
Vest......................				
Trousers......................				
Sweater......................				
Spats......................				
Puttees......................				
Boots......................				
Shoes......................				
Other Articles of the Uniform...				
Skirt (for women).............				

Please indicate as accurately as possible in each column the exact number of instruments furnished by the college or university, the Army, and the students.

KIND OF INSTRUMENT	Number of Instruments Owned by the College That Are Furnished to Students		Number of Instruments Furnished by the Army for R.O.T.C.	Number of Instruments Owned and Used by the Students Themselves
	Free of Charge to Students	Rented to Students		
Piccolo..............................				
Flutes..............................				
Oboes..............................				
English Horn........................				
Sarrusophones......................				
Bassoons...........................				
Eb Clarinets........................				
Bb Clarinets........................				
Alto Clarinets......................				
Bass Clarinets......................				
C Soprano Saxophones...............				
Bb Soprano Saxophones..............				
Alto Saxophones....................				
C Melody Saxophones................				
Tenor Saxophones...................				
Baritone Saxophones................				
BBb Contra Bass Saxophones.........				
French Horns.......................				
Eb Altos—circular and upright.......				
Eb Cornets.........................				
Bb Cornets.........................				
Bb Trumpets........................				
Bb Tenor Trombones—valve and slide ..				
Baritones—single and double bell.......				
Eb Tubas—upright and helicon.........				
BBb Basses —upright and helicon.......				
Snare Drums.......................				
Bass Drums........................				
Tympani (number of drums)..........				
String Basses......................				
Other Instruments..................				

What is the total value of a uniform? $...... Of this total cost how much is furnished by the (College or University? $......) (Army? $......) (Students? $......). How many students have this complete uniform? ....

Out of what fund or funds were the instruments furnished by the college or university purchased?...

....

Out of what fund or funds were the parts of the uniform, indicated as furnished by college, purchased?...

What provision does the college make for purchase of new instruments?

....

For the repair and overhauling of old instruments?......................

....

Who furnishes the funds for band music?................................

Are you limited in the amount that you can spend for music annually? ...... If so what is this amount? $............

Are scholarships or other financial assistance given to band men?.........

How much does this amount to per man per year? $.......

Is added inducement of any kind given to exceptional musicians? ....

....

What does this amount to per year for each man receiving it? $........

Is college or university credit given for band work toward graduation? .... On what degrees is band credit allowed? ....

....

What is the total number of band credits that may be offered toward graduation for the degrees listed above? ....

....

How many hours of credit are given for nine months' work in Band? .....

Is this credit quarter or semester hours? .... What devices do you use for keeping members active in the band the full four years of college?

....

....

How many rehearsals do you have per week? .... How long is each rehearsal (indicate in minutes)? .... What time of day do you hold rehearsal (4:15-5:30 P.M., etc.)? ....

How many weeks do you hold rehearsals regularly during the nine months of school (12 weeks, 24 weeks, 36 weeks, etc.)? ....

INSTRUMENTATION OF BANDS

Place total number of musicians which you have in each band opposite the instruments indicated.

KIND OF INSTRUMENT	Concert Band (not Military or R.O.T.C.)	Second Concert Band	R.O.T.C. or Military Band	Second R.O.T.C. or Military Band
Piccolo				
Flutes				
Oboes				
Bassoons				
English Horns				
Eb Clarinets				
Bb Clarinets				
Alto Clarinets				
Bass Clarinets				
Sarrusophones				
C Soprano Saxophones				
Bb Soprano Saxophones				
Alto Saxophones				
C Melody Saxophones				
Bb Tenor Saxophones				
Baritone Saxophones				
BBb Contra Bass Saxophones				
French Horns				
Eb Altos—circular or upright				
Eb Cornets				
Bb Cornets				
Bb Trumpets				
Tenor Trombones—valve and slide				
Baritones—single and double bell				
Eb Tubas—upright and helicon				
BBb Bases—upright and helicon				
Snare Drums				
Bass Drums				
Tympani				
String Basses				
Other Instruments				
Total number in each band				

What is the total number of *men* in all of the above bands without duplication? ....

Total number of *women* without duplication? ....

Functions at Which the Band Plays Each Year

First .....In Columns I, II, III, and IV place the approximate number of times each year that each band plays at these functions.

Second ...In Column V answer the question "Should any band perform this function in your institution?" Answer by *yes* or *no*.

Third ....In Column VI please indicate which band is best able to serve at each function.

	I	II	III	IV	V	VI
Functions at Which Band Plays	Concert Band (First)	Second Concert Band	R.O. T.C. Band (First)	R.O. T.C. or Military Band (Second)	Should Any Band Perform This Function	
Football Games...............						
Basketball Games.............						
Wrestling Meets..............						
Track Meets..................						
Baseball Games...............						
Pep Meetings.................						
Pep Parades Before or After Games....................						
Political Meetings on Campus..						
Convocations.................						
Assemblies...................						
Graduation Exercises..........						
Spring Open Air Concerts......						
Special Concerts with Paid Admission·..................						
Dedication Exercises All Kinds.						
Spring Carnivals, Campfires or Picnics, etc................						
Other Functions..............						

Were trips taken out of town with athletic teams during the past year? ......

Where? ....

Who paid the expense of the trip? ....

Does your band make a tour? ...... How many days were they on the road last year? .... If possible send itinerary of the last trip? ....

Give dates of concerts given last year at which an admission was charged? ....

If programs of last year's concerts are available please enclose them. ......

Are free open air concerts given as soon as the weather permits in the Spring? ...... How many open air concerts were given last year? ....

Duties of the Officers	Column I	Column II	Column III
Director			
a) Direct the Band at Pep Meetings.............			
b) Political Meeting on Campus.................			
c) Direct the Band at Football Games...........			
d) Direct the Band at Basketball Games.........			
e) Direct the Band at Wrestling Meets...........			
f) Direct the Band at Track Meets..............			
g) Direct the Band at Baseball Games...........			
h) Direct the Band at Convocations..............			
i) Direct the Band at Assemblies			
j) Direct the Band at Graduation Exercises.......			
k) Direct Band on All Out of Town Trips........			
l) Direct Band on Special Concerts			
m) Direct Band on Spring Open Air Concerts......			
n) Direct Band at Dedication Exercises..........			
o) Direct Band at Spring Carnivals, Campfires, etc.			
p) Buy All Music for the Band..................			
q) Buy Instruments and Supplies for the Band			
r) Make Arrangements for Repair of Instruments and Equipment...........................			
s) Make Business Arrangements for Appearances of the Band. Transportation of Men and Instruments......................................			
t) Sell Band Instruments to Band Members......			
u) Recommend Purchase of Instruments and Equipment to the Financial Officer.................			
v) Give Free Band Instruction to Members Who Need It......................................			
w) Give Lessons on Instruments in Music Dept. for Which a Fee is Charged.....................			
x) Complete Charge of Band Each Time it Plays...			
y)			
z)			
Student Director			
a) Direct the Band at Football Games...........			
b) Direct Band at Basketball Games.............			
c) Direct Band at Wrestling Meets..............			
d) Direct Band at Track Meets.................			
e) Direct Band at Baseball Games...............			
f) Direct Band at Convocations.................			
g) Direct Band at Assemblies...................			
h) Direct Band at Graduation Exercises..........			
i) Direct Band at Pep Meetings.................			
j) Direct Band at Pep Parades..................			
k) Direct Band at Open Air Concerts............			
l) Direct Band at Dedication Exercises..........			
m) Make Arrangements for Section Rehearsals.....			

DUTIES OF THE OFFICERS—*Continued*	Column I	Column II	Column III
STUDENT DIRECTOR—*Continued*			
n) Assist Director at Any Time..................			
o) Assume the Duties of Business Manager........			
p) Drill Band for Marching.....................			
q) Direct at Indoor Concerts			
r) Take Roll			
BUSINESS MANAGER			
a) Make Arrangement for Transportation of Men and Instruments at Games...................			
b) Check Band Instruments In and Out..........			
c) Check Uniforms and Equipment In and Out....			
d) Make Arrangements for Commercial Jobs by Band......................................			
e) Make Business Arrangements for Spring Tour ..			
f) Responsible for All Band Equipment..........			
g) Take Roll.................................			
LIBRARIAN			
a) Index and File All Concert Music of Band......			
b) Complete Charge of All Band Music...........			
c) Responsible for Making Up March Books......			
d) Orders Music on Recommendation of Director..			
e) Take Roll.................................			
f) Other Duties..............................			
FIRST CHAIRMAN ON EACH SECTION			
a) Help Others in His Own Section Who Need It...			
b) Hold Special Section Rehearsals When Needed..			
c) Help Director Place Men on Parts............			
d) Other Duties..............................			
DRUM MAJOR			
a) Have Charge of Band at All Times on Parade....			
b) Direct Band in Absence of Director or Student Director...................................			
c) Other Duties..............................			

First .....In Column I, place an X after each duty which in your band is
      now being performed by the officer named.
Second ...Consider ONLY those duties checked in Column I. In Column II
      place a second X after any duty which is checked in Column I,
      but which, in your judgment, *should not be* performed in your
      band by the officer named.

Third .... Consider ONLY those duties which have not been checked at all. In Column III place an X after any such duty which is not checked at all, but which, in your judgment, *should be* performed in your band by the officer named.

Is the Student Director paid for his services? ...... How much does this amount to per year? $........ In your judgment, should he be paid? ...... Is the Librarian paid? ...... How much does this amount to per year? $........ In your judgment, should he be paid? ...... Is the Business Manager paid? ...... How much does this amount to per year? $........ In your judgment, should he be paid? ...... Does the business manager actually handle the money of the band or is it handled through the Bursar's Office? .... Is he required to make a report at regular intervals to the band or Bursar? ....

SUGGESTED CHANGES IN ORGANIZATION OR MANAGEMENT FOR FUTURE IMPROVEMENT OF YOUR BAND

Please indicate any changes in your present organization which would make for greater efficiency, improvement in musical merit, harmony of the organization and service to the institution.
....
                    SIGNED..............................

APPENDIX C–3

SURVEY TO DETERMINE REPLACEMENT AND DEPRECIATION CHARGES FOR UNIFORMS OWNED BY COLLEGE BANDS

Name of Uniform Company...

Date information was returned..

Please answer the following questions on the basis of the uniforms which you manufacture. For example when the question is asked as to the years of service which a band may expect from each article, fill in the number of years of service which bands usually get out of this article which you sell as based on your replacement figures.

In Column I, place the amount which you think is reasonable for annual cleaning and repairing of this article to keep it in good condition.

In Column II, place the average number of years of service which may be expected from this article of the Uniform.

In Column III, place the percentage of the original cost to be charged off as depreciation the first year.

In Column IV, percentage for depreciation the second year.

In Column V, percentage for depreciation the third year.

In Column VI, percentage for depreciation the fourth year.

ARTICLE OF THE UNIFORM	Column I	Column II	Column III	Column IV	Column V	Column VI
Helmet.....................						
Band Cap..................						
Cape.......................						
Coat.......................						
O. D. Army Shirt............						
Trousers...................						
Sweater...................						
Spats......................						
Puttees....................						
Boots......................						
Shoes.....................						
Tuxedo or Full Dress........						
Sam Brown Belt............						
Skirt (for Women)...........						

NOTE—Above list was made up from uniforms indicated by 54 College and University Bands.

APPENDIX D

BIBLIOGRAPHY

BARNES, EDWIN N. C. *Music as an Educational and Social Asset.* Theodore Presser, 1926. 124 pp.

BOURQUIN, MABEL J. "Fostoria High School Band." *Musician,* 27:3, April 1922.

BOUTELLE, G. H. "Economic Value of Music in War." *Bellman,* 23:439-41, Oct. 20, 1917.

BYRN, CLARENCE. "Detroit's All-City High School Band." *Jacobs Band Monthly,* April 1926.

BYRN, CLARENCE. "Public School Training in Vocational Music." *Jacobs Band Monthly,* June 1, 1926.

BYRN, CLARENCE. "The School Band—an Educational Institution." *Jacobs Band Monthly,* January 1926.

CLAPPE, ARTHUR A. *The Band Teacher's Assistant.* Carl Fischer, New York, 1888. 119 pp.

CLUTE, S. "How the School Band Functions." *Musician,* 32:33-39, April 1929.

COGSWELL, H. E. *How to Organize and Conduct the School or Community Band and Orchestra.* J. W. Pepper and Son, Philadelphia, 1919. 72 pp.

EISENBERG, JACOB. "Let us Have a Good Brass Band in Every Community, Says Goldman." *The Musician,* 32:11, April 1927.

———. "Famous Industrial Bands." *Etude,* 41: 368, June 1923.

FISCHER, CHARLES A. "Advertising Value of School Musical Organizations." *Jacobs Band Monthly,* Sept. 1925.

GOLDMAN, EDWIN FRANKO. *Amateur Band Guide and Aid to Leaders.* Carl Fischer, New York, 1916. 144 pp.

GRABEL, V. J. "Appreciation of School Bands." *Etude,* 46:115, 119, Feb.-March, 1928.

GRABEL, V. J. "Bands on Parade." *Etude,* 46:593, Aug.-Sept. 1928.

GRABEL, V. J. "How American Industries are Utilizing Music." *Etude,* 41:303-4, May 1923.

GRABEL, V. J. "Ideals in Band Performance (Preparing for Contests and Concerts)." *Etude,* 46:367, May 1928.

GRABEL, V. J. "The Band as an Important Musical Factor." *Etude,* 46:31, 115, Jan.-Feb. 1928.

———. "Speaking of College Music and Musicians." *Jacobs Band Monthly,* July 1925.

JAMES, LYNN L. "Raising Musicians out Where the West Begins." *Jacobs Band Monthly,* April 1926.

101

KUTSCHINSKI, C. D. "The Winston-Salem Plan, Combining Public School and Community Music." *Jacobs Band Monthly,* March 1925.

LAKE, M. L. *The American Band Arranger.* Carl Fischer, 1920. 44 pp.

LOCKHART, L. M. "College Entrance Requirements and Public School Music." *Jacobs Band Monthly,* October 1925.

LORENZ, CLARICE. "Endowing American Music—an Interview with Agide Facchia." *Jacobs Band Monthly,* April 1926.

MACKIE-BEYER. *The Band Leader's Guide.* J. W. Pepper and Son, Philadelphia.

MACKINTOSH, CHARLES H. *This Age of Rebellion.* Miessner Institute of Music, Milwaukee, 1928. 43 pp.

MADDY, J. E. "How to Develop a School Band." *Etude,* 44:423-4, 569, June-August 1926.

MADDY, J. E. and GIDDINGS, T. P. *Instrumental Technique for Orchestra and Band.* Willis Music Co., Cincinnati, 1926. 255 pp.

MADDY, J. E. *School Bands.* National Bureau for the Advancement of Music, New York, 1927. 31 pp.

MADDY, J. E. "The Wind Band of the Future." *Jacobs Band Monthly,* Feb. 1927.

McCONATHY, OSBOURNE. *Present Status of Music Instruction in Colleges and High Schools,* 1919-1920. Bureau of Education, Washington, D. C., 1921. 54 pp.

MIRICK, G. C. *School Bands, How to Organize and Train Them.* J. W. York, Grand Rapids, Mich., 1924. 31 pp.

ROCHE, L. "The Modern Band." *Etude,* 45:572, Aug. 1927.

RUCKMICK, CHRISTIAN A. "Why an Investment in Music Lessons Always Pays." *Etude,* Jan. 1929.

SCHONEMANN, A. C. E. "Wainwright System of Band Building." *Educational Review,* 69:200-1, April 1925.

STOESSEL, ALBERT. *The Technic of the Baton.* Carl Fischer, New York, 1920. 88 pp.

WAINWRIGHT, J. W. "How to Organize a Boy's High School Band." *Etude,* 42:601-2, Sept. 1924.

WOODS, G. H. *Public School Orchestras and Bands.* Oliver Ditson, Boston, 1922. 204 pp.

VITA

La Verne Buckton was born September 7, 1896, in Iowa Falls, Iowa. He attended the elementary schools and high school of Ames, Iowa. In 1920 he received his B.S. degree from Iowa State College, and in 1921 his M.S. degree from the same institution. In 1928 he received his A.M. degree from Teachers College, Columbia University.

From 1921 to 1924 he was an instructor in the Northfield High School, Northfield, Minnesota. From 1924 to 1926 he was a member of the Vocational Education faculty of Iowa State College. During the Summer Sessions of 1925, 1926, and 1927, he taught at Iowa State College. From the fall of 1928 to the present time, he has been an instructor in education at Hunter College, New York City. At Iowa State College he was elected to Gamma Sigma Delta and was a charter member of Phi Mu Alpha. He was elected to Phi Delta Kappa in 1926 at Teachers College, Columbia University. He received a Lydia C. Roberts Fellowship from Columbia University for the academic years 1926-1927 and 1927-1928. In addition to the present publication he has an unpublished Master's thesis at Iowa State College, "A Course of Study in Vocational Agriculture Based on a Survey of the South Jordan Community." He has published an article "Foreign Languages and the Ph.D.," in the *Journal of Education*, Vol. CII, No. 23, Dec. 24, 1925.